SEVEN DAYS IN
EAST TIMOR

Royalties from this project will be donated to charities relieving the suffering of the people of East Timor and working to rebuild the country.

TIM FISCHER

Ballot and bullets
SEVEN DAYS IN
EAST TIMOR

ALLEN & UNWIN

First published in 2000
Allen & Unwin
9 Atchison Street, St Leonards NSW 1590 Australia
Phone: (61 2) 8425 0100
Fax: (61 2) 9906 2218
E-mail: frontdesk@allen-unwin.com.au
Web: http://www.allen-unwin.com.au

National Library of Australia
Cataloguing-in-Publication entry:

Fischer, Tim, 1946– .
  Seven days in East Timor.

ISBN 1 86508 277 5.

1. Fischer, Tim, 1946– . 2. Australia. East Timor Popular
Consultation. 3. United Nations. Mission in East Timor.
4. Referendum—Indonesia—Timor Timur. 5. Timor Timur
(Indonesia)—History—Autonomy and independence
movements. 6. Timor Timur (Indonesia)—Politics and
government—1966– . I. Title.

959.86039

Set in 12/14 pt Bembo by DOCUPRO, Sydney
Printed and bound by Griffin Press, Adelaide

FOREWORD

FOR 24 YEARS, East Timor was a topic of heated debate between Portugal and Indonesia at the United Nations. It has also been the theme of research papers, seminars, conferences and doctoral theses. Many books and magazine articles have been written on Timor.

However, on the 'H' hour, at the turning point in East Timor's history, no other author has brought to the public mind an account of the Popular Consultation, or referendum, of 30 August 1999.

The publication in Australia of *Seven Days in East Timor: Ballot and Bullets* by the Honourable Tim Fischer, MP, member of the national Parliament of Australia, is indeed very timely.

Mr Fischer describes very vividly and with competence and deep insight, the dramatic events lived by the Timorese people, as well as the expectations and anxieties of all the foreign visitors, including Australia's diplomats. This important event, in which the simple folk of Timor consciously and responsibly decided to turn the winds of time for freedom and independence, will remain as a hallmark in the history of Timor.

I congratulate Tim Fischer in wanting to record for all history the Popular Consultation. And I propose that all Timorese and scholars of Timorese history read *Seven Days in East Timor*, because it is a book that is very useful in understanding the ambitions of both the pro-integration and the pro-independence Timorese and, above all, the Indonesians who foresaw their defeat and departure from Timor after 24 years of oppression and abuse of the fundamental human rights of the Timorese people.

I take this opportunity personally, and on behalf of the Catholics of the Diocese of Dili, to express my deepest thanks to the Australian people for their sympathy and solidarity with the people of Timor, and to the Australian government for making the decisive move in the resolution of the Timorese conflict.

Mgr. Carlos Filipe X.Belo, SDB
Bishop of Dili
Nobel Peace Prize Winner 1996
Dili, 27 November 1999

FOREWORD BY BISHOP BELO   v
MAP OF EAST TIMOR   x
ABBREVIATIONS   xi
ACKNOWLEDGEMENTS   xiii

        INTRODUCTION   1

ONE   THE HOWARD TO HABIBIE LETTER   9

TWO   DESTINATION DARWIN THEN DILI   19
        Thursday 26 August 1999

THREE   BEYOND DILI AND INTO THE BUSH   31
        Friday 27 August 1999

FOUR   TO GLENO AND THE HILLS   42
        Saturday 28 August 1999

FIVE   POLLING DAY EVE   52
        Sunday 29 August 1999

SIX   THE BIG DAY AT LAST   66
        Monday 30 August 1999

SEVEN   RECOVERY DAY   82
        Tuesday 31 August 1999

EIGHT   DEPARTURE FROM DILI   94
        Wednesday 1 September 1999

NINE   THE UGLY POSTSCRIPT   108

TEN   THE MEDIA MAYHEM   119

ELEVEN THE FUTURE   135

INDEX   143

To Judy, Harrison and Dominic

This book is formally dedicated to the people of East Timor who bravely registered and then stepped forward and voted in the popular consultation held on Monday 30 August 1999, and to all those who lost their lives before, during and after the ballot. May they rest in peace.

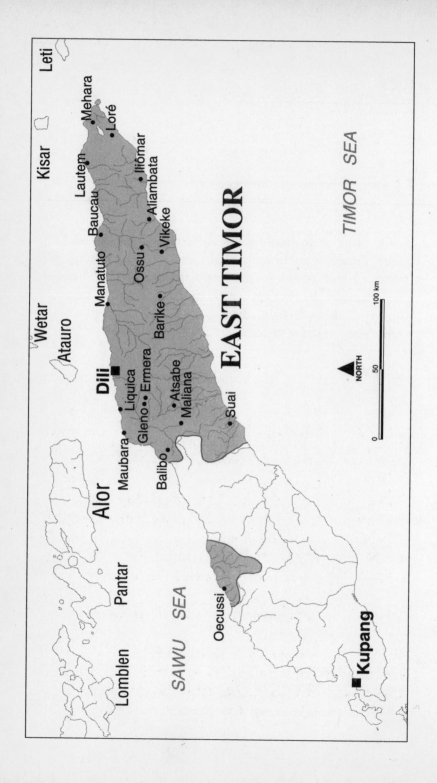

ABBREVIATIONS

ADF	Australian Defence Force
AFP	Australian Federal Police
ANFREL	A Bangkok-based justice organisation
APEC	Asia Pacific Economic Cooperation
ASEAN	Association of South-East Asian Nations
CIVPOL	Civilian Police
CNN	Cable News Network
CNRT	National Council of the Timorese Resistance
DFAT	Department of Foreign Affairs and Trade
IDPs	Internally Displaced People
INTERFET	International Force for East Timor
IORARC	Indian Ocean Rim Association for Regional Cooperation

MPR	People's Consultative Assembly
NGO	Non-government organisation
POLRI	Indonesian Police
RAAF	Royal Australian Air Force
SJ	Society of Jesus
TNI	Indonesian Military
UN	United Nations
UNAMET	United Nations Mission in East Timor
UNIF	The umbrella organisation representing the Pro-Indonesian side
WTO	World Trade Organization

ACKNOWLEDGEMENTS

Whatever the future holds for the people of East Timor, and for those in this part of the world affected by the events there, it is important that the history of this tumultuous period, which culminated in the ballot held on 30 August 1999, be told in as much detail as possible. That is the basis for this project which seeks to record the events I witnessed as leader of the Australian Observer Delegation from 26 August to 1 September 1999.

I acknowledge and thank all the members of the delegation who ensured that our observation of the popular consultation was successful and allowed an accurate record of those observations to be made. The delegation comprised: The Hon Tim Fischer MP; Senator Vicki Bourne; The Hon Laurie Brereton MP; Senator Marise Payne; Mr Kirk Conningham, Mr Anthony Pearce, Ms Stephanie Shwabsky (all from the Department of Foreign Affairs and Trade); Ms Rae Perry representing the Victorian Local Governance Association; Mr Patrick Walsh from the Australian Council for Overseas Aid; and Ms Ann Wigglesworth from Caritas Australia.

I acknowledge and thank Foreign Minister Alexander Downer who appointed the delegation and approved the necessary arrangements.

I also acknowledge and thank, in particular, Ambassador John McCarthy and Consul James Batley and their outstanding and courageous teams, Ian Martin and the UNAMET personnel, Alan Mills and the CIVPOL team, along with the Australian Electoral Commission.

Many others involved should also be thanked, including the ADF personnel, our AFP Security personnel and many East Timorese people from all walks of life.

I also acknowledge the assistance received from some elements of the Indonesian army and police, in particular Lieutenant Arly who helped save Australian lives.

I also want to commend the role of all Australian and international media, with one notable exception, who made heroic efforts to provide essential coverage.

Finally, I especially thank Sue Cox, John Iremonger and Rebecca Kaiser for their guidance and assistance.

This book is sourced from all that I saw first hand in East Timor, and also from non-restricted UN and departmental briefing material and other writings as identified.

INTRODUCTION

*To destroy and exterminate people who oppose inte-
gration. I come carrying the fire of death and I drink
the blood of anti-integrationists. Before you enjoy the results
of the UN and Australian deceit, I will totally destroy you
first until the last. Did you think you could have freedom
without sacrifice? The militia swear they will always defend
the red and white until the last drop of blood.*

This chilling statement by militia leader 'Erico' was
scrawled across the wall of the building next to the
room I occupied in Dili's Hotel Turismo. Discovered
weeks after the ballot, it says much about the end game
agony that descended upon East Timor in September
1999.

After 25 years of pain and little progress on East
Timor, 1999 was to see all of this change with a
sweeping set of developments. The ballot that gave the

people of East Timor a choice about their future brought a brief period of happiness, but it was followed by a time of death and horrific destruction.

My involvement in the ballot started mid year. Just three days after formally ending my tenure as Deputy Prime Minister of Australia and Minister for Trade, I received a message that the Foreign Minister, Alexander Downer, was trying to contact me. It was Friday 23 July and he was in Singapore and as busy as the Foreign Minister is at any time. I thought this was a really nice gesture, that he was obviously wondering how I was surviving my first 72 hours as an ex-minister.

Whilst we had worked closely and smoothly together over five years in our respective portfolios, both in Opposition and after March 1996 in Government, we rarely spoke by phone. As Foreign Minister and Trade Minister we shared the one department, namely Foreign Affairs and Trade (DFAT). This structure worked well as we were in broad agreement on most issues. Departmental procedures saw all paperwork, such as ministerial submissions, reports and cables automatically go to both our offices, so direct ministerial communication was not all that necessary. It did take place, however, when something had to be sorted out at the highest levels.

Needless to say I was wrong about the reason for Alexander's call. He was, in fact, ringing to invite me to lead an official Australian delegation of observers to the East Timor Popular Consultation (to give its correct name). He named the other likely members of the delegation and explained that the task would be difficult and would involve some danger. My wife Judy and I wrestled with this invitation for a day or two, but eventually we decided that I should participate as long as the dates were free of key electorate commitments.

This aspect I finetuned with Michael Smith, Alexander Downer's Chief of Staff.

The ballot had been set down for Monday 30 August and the plan was for the delegation to be in East Timor for about a week. I wanted to delay our departure by a day so that I could spend Wednesday 25 August in Canberra. It was a busy parliamentary sitting day, but I was also due to have a farewell working dinner with the Board of Austrade and this had been organised many weeks before. I did not want to cancel the dinner as under 'Murphy's Law of Ministerial and MP Scheduling' once you juggle a previously agreed to date, the new one never works out. As Austrade had been the cornerstone of the success I was judged to have had in the Trade portfolio, the planned dinner was important to me. So, I figured that by using a RAAF aircraft instead of commercial flights, the delegation would save a day up and back as we could fly directly to Dili and not have to go via Jakarta or Bali. Not only would we save on costs, but we could leave early on Thursday 26 August and I could cover my Austrade obligations.

Once all the scheduling problems were sorted out, I began to think of the invitation as a challenge. Could I handle the role of delegation leader given the diverse membership of the group and could I handle the difficult conditions in East Timor? I figured that this trip could not be any more difficult than the many tight situations I had found myself in over 22 years as a frontbencher in the robust worlds of state and federal politics. So I accepted the position of delegation leader and prepared for the extraordinary seven days I was to spend in Dili and East Timor in August and September 1999.

The popular consultation was the result of an agreement made between the Republic of Indonesia and the Portuguese Republic and a related agreement with the

UN to create UNAMET (United Nations Mission in East Timor). This extraordinary set of documents was signed in New York on the 5 May 1999 by Jaime Gama, the Portuguese Minister for Foreign Affairs, Kofi A. Annan, Secretary-General of the United Nations and Ali Alatas, the Indonesian Minister for Foreign Affairs and provided the basis for the people of East Timor to decide their future: whether they would seek special autonomy under ongoing Indonesian sovereignty, or choose independence involving separate nationhood.

The issues of voter registration, both in East Timor and around the world, and the conduct of the vote were dealt with very broadly in the agreements. However, article number three was very specific. It read, 'The Government of Indonesia will be responsible for maintaining peace and security in East Timor in order to ensure that the popular consultation is carried out in a fair and peaceful way, in an atmosphere free of intimidation, violence or interference from any side'.

To prepare myself for the task of delegation leader, over the next couple of weeks I began to read more closely news items and other material relating to East Timor. I also planned with DFAT that the delegation briefing take place on Monday 23 August at DFAT offices in Canberra, away from Parliament House so we would not be distracted. As a result of my years in public life, I have developed a hatred for having to work and travel on Sunday nights, given that it was usually my one night off for the week. But this was important, so I made a point of arriving in Canberra on Sunday night in order to be at the briefing before 8 am on the Monday morning. This worked out well as I was able to meet those delegation members from the non-government organisations and DFAT officers for a short discussion beforehand and build some rapport with them as delegation leader.

The briefing was comprehensive and delegation members were able to focus on their roles and responsibilities, and take particular regard to the security situation in East Timor. We were warned that Australians had been the subject of considerable hostility and could be targeted one way or the other by the militias and elements of the Indonesian military. Warnings were also issued about malaria and the need to take anti-malaria tablets. It was also confirmed that the ballot would proceed in the Oecussi Enclave (a part of East Timor lying within West Timor) on the same day as elsewhere.

We talked about conditions on the ground in East Timor, the make-up of various groupings and the origins of the quaint term, popular consultation. I recalled Ali Alatas saying at a joint ministerial meeting held between Australia and Indonesia earlier in the year, that the term referendum is simply not well understood in Indonesia. This was echoed by several other Ministers as we spent two days in official talks in Bali at a time when relations were relatively friendly. Using typical diplomatic fudge, it was agreed that in the UN process, the 'referendum' would be called a popular consultation. The results and the decision on the future of East Timor would subsequently have to be ratified by the newly reformed Indonesian parliament, the People's Consultative Assembly (MPR).

While not immediately relevant to the mission before us, we also discussed the Timor Gap Treaty. This had been signed by the then Australian Minister for Foreign Affairs, Gareth Evans, and Ali Alatas in 1989. It provided for the carve up of the oil and gas reserves of the Timor Gap into three zones with the billions of dollars worth of potential royalties being allocated to both Australia and Indonesia. At our ministerial meeting in Bali, Ali Alatas and Coordination Minister Dr Ginangar very clearly stated that with independence Indonesia would step out of the Timor Gap Treaty and East Timor would step in. Alexander Downer fleshed this out further, affirming that Australia was not seeking to increase its share of Timor Gap oil reserves. Under the principle relating to successor States, there would be no change in the various arrangements and boundaries laid out by the Treaty.

The briefing ended with the reminder that there would be no scope for individual activities and itineraries and that we would have to support one another at all times.

I left the briefing room feeling very subdued. I was conscious that this delegation faced a pretty difficult time with challenging situations and conditions awaiting us. Nevertheless, I appreciated the task of observing this important ballot was a vital and worthy one. The dangers we were to face would be nowhere near as great as for those staying on in East Timor after the ballot was announced.

The delegation represented a wide cross-section of political opinion. Over the years I had come to know the ways of a number of my parliamentary colleagues now on the delegation. Sometimes I had clashed with them. This was especially true of the ALP's Laurie Brereton as we sat opposite one another in the Lower House. You move on from these spats, but the very different personalities on the delegation would require careful handling.

Laurie Brereton had been in New South Wales and Federal Parliament for over 25 years and as Shadow Minister of Foreign Affairs he was keen to be seen as being active. If this meant scoring points against Alexander Downer, so be it. New South Wales Liberal Senator Marise Payne, on the other hand, had been in the Senate for only two years. She was ready to work hard and scrutinise carefully. Senator Vicki Bourne, a senior Democrats Senator also from New South Wales, had consistently supported East Timor independence and had followed the issues very closely over the years.

Adding diversity were the delegation members who were neither Federal or State parliamentarians. Rae Perry was a local government representative. An ALP councillor, she was not factionally aligned, and had a friendly manner and plenty of energy. The wise and determined Patrick Walsh was a senior representative from the Australian Council for Overseas Aid, and Ann Wigglesworth had been to East Timor before working with Caritas Australia, the Catholic relief agency which ran health and education programs in East Timor. The DFAT officers, Stephanie Shwabsky, Kirk Conningham and Anthony Pearce were very competent in their different ways and were not without humour. This assortment of people from many backgrounds shared one common thread, a strong belief in the importance of a free and fair ballot.

We were to work closely with UNAMET, the organisation with overall responsibility for the conduct of the ballot, so in our preparations and briefings we were given detailed information about its role. There were issues to consider relating to security and the operational conduct of the ballot such as the delivery of 850 ballot boxes, the printing of the roll of registered voters and the introduction of polling place arrangements that ensured secrecy. We were told that UNAMET was being supported by a strong but unarmed military liaison unit, which had headquarters up the hill from UNAMET's main Dili compound. There was also the large CIVPOL unit, made up of civilian police from many countries, again unarmed, and scattered across various centres, both large and small, throughout East Timor.

It was also explained that UNAMET's electoral

officers came from around the world, but that they were being helped by many locally engaged staff. Overseeing proceedings were the three electoral commissioners— one each from Ireland, Korea and South Africa. The Australian Electoral Commission was also playing a huge supporting role by helping to provide computer printed rolls and other material.

With briefing notes read, malaria tablets packed and desks cleared, we were ready to join observers, journalists, electoral officers and aid workers from around the world to watch either the birth of a new nation or the final and complete incorporation of East Timor into Indonesia.

ONE

THE HOWARD TO HABIBIE LETTER

IN DECEMBER 1998 the Federal Government was wind-ing down for the summer break after a frenetic year that had included the long build-up to the Federal election held on 3 October 1998. The Liberal and National Party Coalition had been returned to govern-ment but with a reduced majority on the floor of the Lower House with the Democrats holding the balance of power in the Senate. The One Nation bandwagon led by Pauline Hanson had been derailed, and she lost her seat in the House of Representatives. Her party failed to win any other seats in the Lower House, but did capture one Senate seat.

After the Coalition win, key party meetings elected John Howard as Leader of the Liberal Party and so continuing as Prime Minister, and me as Leader of the National Party and therefore Deputy Prime Minister. A major Cabinet reshuffle took place at the same time with John Moore being appointed to the key portfolio of Defence, and John Anderson taking the portfolio of Transport and Regional Services (a name change I had suggested from Regional Development). Alexander Downer continued as Minister for Foreign Affairs and I continued as Minister for Trade, squeezing in a quick working visit to Argentina, Chile and Uruguay in November 1998.

There was a good deal of exhaustion in the ranks. Just about everyone was of the view that the Christmas break, including the few weeks summer recess, could not come quickly enough. This was not, however, the case with some sections of the Government who were very busy, driving forward a proposal that culminated in a formal letter from Prime Minister John Howard to Indonesian President Habibie.

This three-page letter, which John Howard signed on 19 December 1998, was to become one of the catalysts that caused Indonesia to change longstanding policy and bring forward a choice for the people of East Timor. The Prime Minister wrote the salutation 'My Dear President' in his own hand to the letter which read:

> It was good to meet you in Kuala Lumpur and hear of the progress you are making with your political and economic reform program. I have followed with particular interest the development of your plans for elections next year and am pleased that our Electoral Commission has recently been in Indonesia discussing ways in which we can help you with them.
>
> You have an enormous amount on your agenda and East Timor is just one of many pressing issues. But I hope that, recognising our goodwill towards you personally and towards Indonesia, you will permit me to make some suggestions about the East Timor situation.

Your offer of autonomy for East Timor was a bold and clear-sighted step that has opened a window of opportunity both to achieve a peaceful settlement in East Timor and to resolve an issue that has long caused Indonesia difficulties in the international community. A settlement would enable you to put the issue behind you. It would make a substantial difference to Indonesia's standing in the world, with the benefits that could bring.

I want to emphasise that Australia's support for Indonesia's sovereignty is unchanged. It has been a longstanding Australian position that the interests of Australia, Indonesia and East Timor are best served by East Timor remaining part of Indonesia. We would of course welcome any peaceful settlement that had the support of both Indonesians and East Timorese and met the interests and aspirations of both.

Observing the developments since your offer of autonomy, however, I fear that the boldness of your offer has not been matched with the degree of progress in negotiations which might have been expected. My concerns are that the UN process is not producing the desired results quickly enough, and that, with heightened expectations, attitudes in East Timor are hardening. It would be a real tragedy if the opening you have created is not taken advantage of and the situation worsens in East Timor.

In our view, one reason for the difficulties is that negotiations with the Portuguese do not give an adequate role for the East Timorese themselves. In the end, the issue can be resolved only through direct negotiations between Indonesia and East Timorese leaders. If you can reach agreement directly with the East Timorese, then the international dimensions would take care of themselves, or at least be much easier to deal with.

I would urge you to take this course, and to focus on winning acceptance for your offer from the East Timorese themselves. The best way of achieving this may be for you to enter into direct negotiations with representative leaders from East Timor, including the two East Timorese bishops and Xanana Gusmao.

On the substance of the negotiations, the advice I am receiving is that a decisive element of East Timorese opinion is insisting on an act of self-determination. If anything, their position—with a fair degree of international support—seems to be strengthening on this.

It might be worth considering, therefore, a means of addressing the East Timorese desire for an act of self-determination in a manner that avoids an early and final decision on the future status of the province. One way of doing this would be to build into the autonomy package a review mechanism along the lines of the Matignon Accords in New Caledonia. The Matignon Accords have enabled a compromise political solution to be implemented while deferring a referendum on the final status of New Caledonia for many years.

The successful implementation of an autonomy package with a built-in review mechanism would allow time to convince the East Timorese of the benefits of autonomy within the Indonesian Republic.

I take the liberty of making these suggestions, knowing the matter is complex and not pretending to have the solutions. I hope, however, that some of these outside perspectives might be useful to you in your efforts to reach a settlement.

Australia wants very much to see a just and lasting solution to the problem. We believe that a solution is within your grasp if the visionary lead you have given can be followed up effectively and directly with the East Timorese.

If you see any merit in these thoughts I would be happy to talk with you directly about them or have some one discuss them discreetly with you. We are very willing to do what we can to help.

This letter was a carefully constructed initiative to move forward on a proposition which had, in one form or another, been discussed for some time in various corridors of power, particularly in Portugal and the rest of Europe. Hand delivered to the President by Australian Ambassador John McCarthy, it was an attempt to address the East Timor issue which had, since 1975, remained unresolved in the eyes of many around the world, especially in Portugal, the colonial power that had ruled East Timor for over 400 years.

Throughout 1998, Foreign Minister Alexander Downer and the Department of Foreign Affairs and Trade, at various levels from the Departmental Secretary Dr Ashton Calvert down, had been considering ideas that might move the East Timor agenda forward. After the October elections, these ideas were developed further and crystallised in the letter proposal that Alexander Downer took to the Prime Minister. The Prime Minister's Foreign Affairs Adviser, Michael Thawley, and others in the Department of Prime Minister and Cabinet, also became involved in finetuning the proposal. I am not able to say what deliberations took place within the Cabinet or the National Security Committee, but what is on the public record is clear enough. A number of ideas were canvassed in the aftermath of President Habibie's offer of autonomy for East Timor and this led to the Prime Minister signing the letter on 19 December 1998.

It was a 'big call' by all who were directly involved, particularly John Howard. Here was the Australian Prime

Minister writing to the Indonesian President suggesting a way forward within a context that acknowledged Australia's support for Indonesian sovereignty over East Timor remained unchanged. The issues raised in the letter made their way on to the public record in one form or another throughout the second half of 1999.

The letter, despite its gentle presentation of a solution to the East Timor issue, caused consternation in Jakarta. Indonesia's Foreign Minister, Ali Alatas, said that the letter had angered President Habibie because it had come from Australia. There was concern that East Timor would take Indonesian subsidies through a long period of autonomy and then seek independence. 'It was no wonder that Habibie then said that maybe we need an alternative', Dr Alatas later explained. (There is some doubt as to the extent of Habibie's anger, but other key players in Jakarta were unimpressed.)

The letter was diplomatic dynamite, so it was inevitable that knowledge of it would surface publicly. In fact, details of the letter 'leaked' in the middle of the following month in the *Australian*. It was undoubtedly a scoop for that newspaper's Jakarta correspondent at the time, Don Greenlees, and Canberra correspondent, Richard McGregor. (The *Australian* subsequently put the whole letter on its web page.) In the aftermath of the leak, an Indonesian foreign affairs spokesman expressed concern and deep regret about Australia's change in policy approach. The spokesman in a statement believed to have been dictated by Ali Alatas, who was in transit at the time, said the Australian move would have an adverse affect on negotiations over the detail of arrangements for a 'people's choice' in East Timor. Alexander Downer deferred his leave for one day to handle the Australian media. In his comments Minister Downer said it was a significant shift reflecting the new situation and a change in dynamics.

An intense 'behind the scenes' debate proceeded in Jakarta where for some time a view had been growing among Indonesian elites that East Timor was costing too much money, that no real progress was being made in establishing Indonesia's sovereignty in an acceptable manner, and that the whole business was commanding too much in time and diplomatic and military resources. President Habibie eventually came to the conclusion that if there was to be a vote allowing choice in East Timor, why not have that vote sooner rather than later? Without a resolution Indonesia could continue to spend a huge amount of money and invest resources on East Timor only to see that province depart in five or ten years time. This view also held sway with some members of the Indonesian Army. Even General Wiranto was quoted as saying that he supported the conduct of a 'popular consultation'.

The Howard to Habibie letter worked, at least to the extent of breaking the stalemate over East Timor. It was a bold letter by a prime minister at the very start of his second term, an initiative with many risks and many ramifications. Indeed, it may take many years to work out the full impact of John Howard's letter and perhaps at some future date it will be equated with such famous letters as the Balfour letter to Lord Rothschild, written on 2 November 1917. Arthur Balfour was the British Government Foreign Secretary when he wrote:

> His Majesty's Government view with favour the establishment in Palestine of a national home for the Jewish people, and will use their best endeavours to facilitate the achievement of this object, it being clearly understood that nothing shall be done which may prejudice the civil and religious rights of existing non-Jewish communities in Palestine, or the rights and political status enjoyed by Jews in any other country. I

should be grateful if you would bring this declaration to the knowledge of the Zionist Federation.

Both letters were to contribute to the establishment of independent nations. While the Balfour letter and subsequent declaration may have played a more seminal role in creating Israel than the Howard letter eight decades later, the importance of the Prime Minister's letter should not be underestimated.

President Habibie received the letter at a time when there was opportunity for change due, in particular, to two factors. The first was personal. President Habibie had spent many years as a young man working with Messerschmitt in Germany, a democracy that placed a high value on human rights. As president, he was not wedded to the hardline military beliefs that had pushed Indonesian expansion over the years and drove the invasion of East Timor in 1975. Here was a President prepared to listen to those in the business community, to those in civil society, with their growing view that enough was enough on the question of East Timor.

Second, the Indonesian Army itself was off balance, having lost its patron, the former general and extremely long-serving national leader, President Soeharto. Also the Indonesian Army, like other armies in Southeast Asia, had suffered greatly from the Asian economic meltdown, which began to have its major impact from June 1997. Budget allocations were cut and the buying power of the national currency greatly reduced thus limiting overseas equipment and maintenance contract purchases. The commercial activities of the Army (and of individual generals who were supplementing their low official pay through business activities) also became seriously affected. Some generals moved quickly, and switched their reserves of local currency into US dollars and other hard currencies, and parked large amounts of

money in Singapore and/or Switzerland. The conse-
quence of all of this was a somewhat weakened senior
echelon of the Indonesian Army that no longer had the
ability to veto key aspects of Government policy.

It is testimony to the fact that there was some depth
in Australia and Indonesia's bilateral relationship that
Jakarta did not tear up the letter on the spot. For all the
harsh criticisms and sparks between Australia and Indonesia over the years, greatly leveraged by the media in
both countries, there is a degree of underlying goodwill
that should not be understated and that will return when
things calm down. Part of the problem is a feeling in
Indonesia that Australia seeks to apply ridiculously high
standards of governance to issues. Also, Indonesia fails to
understand Australia's approach to freedom of the press,
which often results in free-wheeling criticisms of some of
Asia's sacred cows. The rush to judgement in Australia
over developments in Indonesia is often resented, adding
difficulty to the management of bilateral relations. These
relations are best based on mutual respect and in working
hard at understanding one another's culture and priorities.

While the Howard to Habibie letter injected some
tension into the relationship, its timing had been about
right. If it had been sent any earlier, it would have failed
because President Soeharto would not have accepted any
form of choice, including a popular consultation, for the
people of East Timor, and the Army would have closely
followed the same line. If the letter had been sent any
later, after Habibie's presidency had ended, it would
have also failed. Abdurrahman Wahid and Megawati
Sukarnoputri, who were to be elected President and
Vice-President of Indonesia in October 1999, had both
expressed strong support for the unity of Indonesia and
its 27 provinces during their campaigns. They were
opposed to any splintering of the giant archipelago that
made up Indonesia. It was therefore only in the middle

of Habibie's presidential term that there was some scope to nudge forward a genuinely reforming agenda on East Timor.

So, we entered 1999 with the letter signed, sealed and delivered. The economies of Asia were starting to recover from the meltdown of 1997. Indonesia, Thailand and Korea had each received a one billion dollar Australian currency facility to help stabilise things during the meltdown. Federal Cabinet made these approvals, which were only partially taken up, with care and it was heartening to see real signs of economic growth emerging across most of Asia in 1999. Australia had no particular leverage over Indonesia as a result of this financial assistance. The help was well intentioned and the correct call. Diplomatic relations between Australia and Indonesia were still in place and there was a degree of progress on the future of East Timor, something that we had not seen over the previous quarter of a century.

This was how things stood when I received that telephone call from Alexander Downer.

TWO

DESTINATION DARWIN THEN DILI

Thursday 26 August 1999

T HERE COULD BE no turning back. I was now locked
in to a week in East Timor and all it might mean.
This was my overriding and grim thought as the RAAF
Falcon jet commenced its descent into Dili. We broke
through a layer of light cloud and immediately spotted
the huge statue of Jesus Christ dominating the headland
just east of Dili. This extraordinary statue faces west in
the direction of both Jerusalem and Jakarta. Built on the
order of former Indonesian President Soeharto, it was
a somewhat bizarre but welcoming sign to the ballot
and battles that lay ahead for East Timor.

In the distance the mountains quickly climbed to
over 2000 metres to make up the main spine of Timor.
Immediately before us, between mountain and sea, was
the city of Dili where no building appeared over four
storeys high. There was a reasonably standard crisscross-
ing of streets and the odd church stood out. Through
the smoke and haze we could see an idyllic island or

two to the north. I was not feeling at all nervous, although I was a little tired after the late night and early start from Canberra. It was exciting to have finally made it to East Timor.

Back in Canberra earlier that morning there had been no fog. I took this as a good omen for the official Australian Observer Delegation. And, unusually for a group of parliamentarians, all the members of the delegation had arrived on time.

En route to Dili via Darwin I made a point of talking to each member of the delegation and with Craig Jacobsen and Paul Cartwright, officers from the Australian Federal Police who were not only assigned to offer us protection on the ground in East Timor, but had a more strategic role as well, as I was to learn later.

I distributed some talking points to help guide delegation members when dealing with the ever-present and all important media. This was especially important for the doorstop question-and-answer session scheduled during our refuelling stop at the Darwin RAAF Base. I realised Laurie Brereton, as Shadow Minister for Foreign Affairs, would be 'pushing the envelope' at every opportunity and that Rae Perry, Patrick Walsh and Ann Wigglesworth, the three non-government officers, would have their own firm views coming as they did from advocacy organisations.

Given that Indonesia had refused to issue Laurie Brereton a visa to visit East Timor earlier in the year, I was urging on him a degree of caution in his public utterances lest we be blocked by the Indonesians and turned back at Dili Airport. For whatever reason, Laurie was careful and he pulled back to a degree from his earlier attacks and provocative statements.

I was slightly nervous about holding this group together after hearing about the nightmare trip of an All Party delegation to Africa several years ago. Civil relations within the delegation broke down country by country, with delegation members openly fighting with each other in front of bemused African presidents and prime ministers. This led to a famous cartoon showing a bundle of Australian MPs descending from an aircraft with a confused general looking apprehensively from behind his hand of salute.

I wanted to avoid such a breakdown of relations at all costs as it would add to the burden of hard-pressed staff at the Dili Consulate and would prevent the delegation from doing its prime task, namely to accurately observe and monitor the ballot. However, I did wonder whether or not this East Timor delegation would end up being a repeat of that disastrous African delegation. On balance, I thought there was too much at stake for the group to allow this to happen. But I vowed to quietly work to ensure the delegation held together and did the job it was meant to do.

Needless to say, the large media turnout at the Darwin RAAF base had plenty of questions to ask, but it especially focused on the ballot and the security concerns. This was my first doorstop since stepping down as Deputy Prime Minister and Minister for Trade over a month before. I found myself to be a little rusty in handling the quick-fire questions from the media, but was able to break off without any obvious disasters and move into the RAAF Headquarters terminal where we completed final immigration and customs clearances.

I have always found the varied tasks associated with being a Member of Parliament greatly stimulating. From chairing conferences in capital cities to inspecting a drainage problem out the back of Bourke, this variety has helped outweigh the dreary side and demanding schedules of political life. So I was happy to swing into a committee room to receive a mini delegation wanting to discuss ways of boosting Australia's live cattle trade to the north.

I had arranged this meeting to save the exporters the cost of coming to Canberra. It was an extraordinary last meeting on Australian soil before the week in Dili and East Timor given that it was in such stark contrast to the role I was taking on as delegation leader. I suggested some action that could be taken through the office of the new Minister for Trade, Mark Vaile. It was then all aboard for our last leg to Dili.

Flying past that statue of Jesus Christ and the peaceful looking centre of Dili, we turned sharply to land. Dili Airport is strategically located just west of the town, on land adjoining the sea. The one runway virtually starts and ends at the water's edge meaning all aircraft make their final approach over water. I noted that this greatly reduced exposure of aircraft to attack and restricted small-arms fire being directed at low flying aircraft. It was a comforting thought.

On arrival in the early afternoon, we were met by Australia's Ambassador to Indonesia, John McCarthy, and Consul in East Timor, James Batley. We were grateful that John, James and their team were cool, calm and professional in the hot and difficult conditions. I suggested to John that as the successful 'Ambassador from Central Casting' (a compliment used to describe him years ago), he probably hadn't planned this particular role in East Timor.

There was no doubt John McCarthy was one of our most experienced and professional ambassadors with his many postings as Head of Mission, including to Bangkok and Washington. He knew the Asian way of doing things very well, but had not fallen for the mistake of immersing himself so much in local culture as to lose sight of Australia's priorities. He was a very dedicated

Ambassador to Indonesia who had made many trips to East Timor.

John smiled wryly at the jibe about Central Casting as he ushered us into a VIP lounge to await the arrival of the Governor of East Timor. It was in the waiting room that we heard the first of many conflicting reports of trouble taking place in downtown Dili, involving rioting and shooting and the burning of buildings.

The Indonesian controlled administration had allowed the groups who supported special autonomy for East Timor to conduct their final rallies that afternoon. As we landed we had seen convoys of trucks loaded with hundreds of people waving red and white Indonesian flags, all of whom were obviously part of the autonomy rallies.

When Governor Abilio Jose Osorio Soares eventually arrived, he was polite and welcoming, but I thought a little reserved and tense, even allowing for the formality of local custom and practice. Reports of the trouble in Dili were enough to have us tread warily as we spoke with him. (At this stage we weren't even aware of the allegations that plans had been drawn up in February 1999 to massacre pro-independence East Timorese or of the orders to kill priests and nuns where survivors of the militia attacks went into churches and the homes of priests for refuge.)

I led the discussions which again focused on security arrangements for the people of East Timor, particularly on ballot day. The Governor gave the appropriate responses that the safety of the people of East Timor would be assured, but he was guarded and distant. I wondered if I had been too direct, as I often can be in Asia, having to correct myself and ease back. I later checked with others who thought the discussion had been okay, but clearly the Governor was under some pressure. In any event, he had a plane to catch to Jakarta and soon hastened away but not before reiterating that Indonesia would stand by the ballot and accept the voters' decision.

As we loaded into vehicles for the short trip into town, I held another quick doorstop and realised that there was going to be a huge media frenzy over the next few days. Would this wall to wall international media coverage help keep violence in check and allow the ballot to proceed peacefully? Maybe.

It seems that all good cities must have one relatively grand roundabout just near the airport. So it was in Dili. Although not as grand as the arch and roundabout near Teheran Airport, Dili's roundabout was decorated for the 50th Anniversary of Indonesia's independence, a celebration that had taken place a few days before.

We crossed a long bridge with steel girders over a dry riverbed, drove past the Australian Consulate, the ferry wharf and the main government buildings to arrive at Hotel Turismo, one of only three hotels operating in Dili.

The Hotel Turismo was a two storey concrete building with a central foyer and dining room on the ground floor. There were two garden courtyards, one large and one small, with some tables and chairs. Whilst all the bedrooms were of adequate size, the bathrooms were tiny and on first glance the plumbing looked somewhat ancient and therefore dubious.

I checked into Room 38 and was greatly relieved to discover that I would not have to share. I would have the space that my eldest son Harrison sometimes reminds me he needs. As there would be no chance to break away from the delegation, I certainly valued the privacy the room offered. I would be able to ring my wife Judy and my family without disturbing anybody else, and I would have the chance to write up my diary and reflect on the events of each day.

We moved in convoy to our appointment with the Indonesian Police Colonel Timbul Silaen. Some of our escort and security personnel passed on fresh reports of violence in downtown Dili. A distant rumble could be heard and some shots were fired as we were ushered into the surreal atmosphere of the police conference room.

I led some direct questioning about what was happening in Dili that afternoon, only to be given an obscure reply about the premises of a small business being burnt and stones being thrown. My colleagues joined in the discussion, and again we received all the right assurances. Colonel Silaen emphasised that the Indonesian Government had deployed 8000 police for the popular consultation and the Indonesian Military (TNI) had some 10 000 troops on the ground in East Timor to guarantee the safety of the East Timorese.

I looked across the room as these figures, and much else besides, were being bandied around. I remember seeing a cabinet full of trophies that members of the Indonesian Police Force in East Timor had no doubt won in sporting and other police competitions. Some things are the same the world over.

Colonel Silaen was not a happy person. To be fair his unhappiness was not directed at us, but at the whole raft of events he had to handle. He seemed extremely tired and looked even wearier when I caught up with him again four days later. He did not have any additional late-breaking information on the events in downtown Dili.

The delegation moved on to Army Headquarters to meet with the then Military Commander for East Timor, Colonel Mohamed Noer Muis, and Jakarta-appointed ambassador, Agus Tarmidzi, head of the Indonesian Task Force that had some responsibility for the implementation of the popular consultation. Colonel

Muis was a cool customer and reasonably fresh to the task as he was newly appointed. In 1993 he had been a staff college classmate at Queenscliff in Victoria with Lieutenant Colonel Paul Symon, the senior Australian Army officer working with UNAMET on the ground in East Timor. I thought this might help build our relationship and for a period it did. Unfortunately, elements of the militia were to ultimately overwhelm the command control of the TNI in the aftermath of the ballot. Mind you, the militia did as they pleased even before the ballot despite the various high-level assurances we were given about peace and security.

Commander Muis and the Special Ambassador Tarmidzi both expected a fair consultation on 30 August and were encouraging a peaceful atmosphere, free from intimidation. They emphasised that the police, the TNI, UNAMET and, looking at us, domestic and international observers would need to be neutral. I confirmed that the Australian Observer Delegation would comply with the guidelines and would not take sides as it observed the various procedures associated with the ballot. No mention was made of Kopassus, the special forces unit of the Indonesian Army roughly equivalent to the Australian Special Air Services. Kopassus was responsible for para-commando operations and anti-terrorist operations and was said to have strong links with the militia. It needed to be watched closely.

After these meetings, our security detail informed us of trouble on the nearby streets of Dili. I saw two clusters of Indonesian Police in flak vests and with a full array of protection equipment, but they were some distance from where the worst incidents had occurred that afternoon. The office of the CNRT (National Council of the Timorese Resistance) and a number of other buildings and houses had been burnt and several people killed. CNN had graphically filmed the destruction as heavily armed militia gangs surged forward waving guns and huge machetes, and went on a firing rampage into a house near the UNAMET compound. For the sin of displaying a photo of Xanana Gusmao inside their front door, an elderly couple was shot dead.

Up to ten people were reported to have been killed by militias in Dili on that angry afternoon. Even non-Timorese were not protected against the rampage as militias climbed a fence and attacked the Hotel Dili, and later fired at journalists. However, in other parts of Dili the streets were almost empty and, in sharp contrast to the murder and mayhem elsewhere, totally tranquil.

Sunset brought calm, and back in the Hotel Turismo we were advised that we should not go out again that night. We would stay in and enjoy whatever the hard pressed staff of the hotel could give us for dinner.

That night we watched journalists monitor the CNN crosses to East Timor so they could crosscheck their own stories. Staying at Hotel Turismo were some larger than life reporters with extraordinary tales to tell. The colourful Australia-based correspondent for the Spanish International News Agency, Carlos Rubio, was a recent arrival. He had not unreasonably taken objection to having a gun pointed at him by militia who had stormed through the Hotel Dili as part of that afternoon's melee. At one stage, Carlos and three other journalists were pinned against a wall of the hotel by a young militiaman seemingly high on drugs. The militiaman waved his gun directly at the four for a couple of minutes and screamed 'I hate you' and 'I want to kill you' as the blood vessels in his neck swelled up. With their lives seemingly in the balance, the four sweating journalists held up their hands and urged their assailant to calm down. The seconds ticked away when a senior militiaman suddenly appeared telling the young man to move on.

Carlos was deeply shaken. He had feared for his life

and with the other journalists eventually managed to get out of the Hotel Dili to be escorted to the relative safety of the Hotel Turismo, where he calmed down from his searing experiences.

In all crises there are always moments of humour and it was the young dark-haired Carlos asking if anyone had a spare bed that lightened the mood that night. Some of the women journalists joked that they were more than happy to give Carlos a bed so that he would not have to sleep in the gutter. However, in truth, romance was the last thing on his mind. He was so upset by all he had seen that day, he was seeking help to get out of East Timor. Carlos had had enough. I made some inquiries to ensure that he'd be able to catch a commercial flight out of Dili. When in Sydney Carlos was based in the Eastern Suburbs. We agreed that Bondi and Bronte beaches were looking a whole lot more attractive than Dili Beach at this time. Carlos told me later that he ended up sharing with an ugly British journalist who reminded him of Don Quixote, but he was grateful for the help.

The Australian Ambassador, John McCarthy, had monitored the worsening security situation throughout the day and held a special briefing that night at the Hotel Turismo. We all crowded into Fairfax journalist Lindsay Murdoch's first floor room as the ambassador explained evacuation arrangements and the state of play as it was known at that time. Remembering what happened during the fall of Saigon in 1975, some journalists said that Australia should not make the mistake of leaving behind locally engaged staff should there be an emergency evacuation.

It had been a long day that started some eighteen hours earlier in the cocoon of Canberra during a parliamentary sitting week. As I thought about the agony occurring on the streets of Dili, I began to fully realise how wild the set of cards stacked against holding the ballot on time were, let alone what might happen in the aftermath of the ballot. I searched for reasons for optimism knowing that less than one kilometre from where I slept, killings and destruction had been allowed to take place in the heat of the afternoon. Would the forces in favour of disruption back off if they thought they still had a chance of winning over 50 per cent of the votes to the pro-autonomy cause?

We were not told about what had happened on the streets of Dili by those who had responsibility for monitoring and controlling the situation. Worse still, with the Indonesian Army and Police contingents in their thousands, there were clearly the resources to stop the violence. When we met the Governor at the airport earlier that day, he may have only had an inkling of what was occurring on the streets. On the other hand, the three senior Indonesian officials we spoke to either knew or should have known, but said nothing to us.

How deliberate this was, I don't know. But I did recall that some Indonesian military and police units had a reluctance to pass bad news up the chain of command, a cultural phenomenon not unknown in some large organisations in Australia and other parts of the world. So, perhaps, in fairness the three senior Indonesian officials simply did not know the details of the violence that took place virtually under their noses, or at least until they turned on that night's CNN news.

Still, I had an uneasy feeling that on our first day in East Timor, the delegation may have been duped or misled not once, or twice, but thrice! I silently vowed to be on the look out and to ask all of the right questions in the meetings that lay ahead, but in a way that did not give unnecessary offence. Over my years as Minister for Trade, I had developed some skill in doing this, but the challenge here would be to carry out this task in very difficult circumstances.

Thanks to the good work of all of those involved with security, at no stage during the day did I think we had been in any personal danger. To some extent there was a great element of luck in this and we were helped by an unwritten rule applying at the time to Westerners. We were to be spared, at least for now, even though we could have been attacked with ease. Sadly, it seemed, this rule wasn't to be applied to the East Timorese, who were seen as fair targets and whose lives were valued cheaply. This left me sad and with a dry taste in my mouth.

Before trying to get some sleep that night, I dived under a thin stream of water that was an apology for a shower, forgetting that only cold water was available. After two minutes I stepped out quietly furious that I was wide awake again at midnight. So I flicked on the TV to unwind and incredibly there was a choice of channels available in this tiny Dili hotel room—CNN and BBC World Service along with Indonesian channels and Australia Television International, now owned by Channel 7 and playing a vital role in bringing news to the people of Indonesia by way of ABC TV news replays.

Day one ended with the delegation working increasingly well together despite the tension around Dili and all that had happened in East Timor that afternoon.

My last thought was of Kopassus, the hard edge to the Indonesian Army. Surely they could keep control? And then the penny dropped. If, in fact, Kopassus was resupplying the militia or worse, was still swapping shirts with them to do some of the killing, the militia would never be fired on. Ugh I thought, and dozed off.

THREE

BEYOND DILI AND INTO
THE BUSH

Friday 27 August 1999

A NEW DAY DAWNED peacefully enough. I had a one egg breakfast in the crowded dining- come multi-purpose room on the ground floor of the Hotel Turismo. It was always a noisy place with CNN on every minute of the day. Any attempt to alter the sound level was always howled down for concern that an update on East Timor might be missed.

A UNAMET chartered Hercules on a regular run between Darwin and Dili flew past, just out to sea. It was followed by an Iroquois helicopter which flew low, almost overhead the Hotel Turismo. I closed my eyes and thought for a moment that I was back in Vietnam thirty years ago. There is nothing more distinctive than the sound of the helicopter blades of an Iroquois. In Vietnam, it was by and large a welcoming sound as it meant food and ammunition resupply was on the way, perhaps some letters from home, or even an easy evacuation back to base instead of a long foot slog.

I reminded myself that this was not Vietnam and that the obvious mistakes made there should not be repeated in East Timor. This required that a full and fair ballot take place with absolute integrity so that the will of the people of East Timor could be established, one way or the other. It also required that their choice be implemented as quickly and as peacefully as possible.

We had already decided that to understand the situation beyond Dili, the delegation would be split today, with one group moving east to the important town of Baucau and the other group travelling west of Dili to Liquica, a hotspot on the coast. As delegation leader I thought I should go to where the militia were known to be particularly active, but the hotspots were both west and east. It was agreed, after further discussion, that the group going east would be led by Marise Payne and would comprise Vicki Bourne, Pat Walsh, Ann Wigglesworth and Kirk Conningham, together with a security detail. I led the group that went west and this included Laurie Brereton, Rae Perry, Stephanie Shwabsky and Anthony Pearce along with another small security detail.

We departed Dili midmorning and in a small convoy headed past the airport along the coast road. We passed a fishing village and encountered scenes of absolute tranquillity in the warmth of the late morning. Many East Timorese were lying on mats sleeping, perhaps after a busy period of dawn fishing. The road crept along the edge of rugged hills which ran up to nearby mountain ranges, and between the coast and the mountains lay a narrow strip of level land. There was a similarity to the north coast of Crete, but I was surprised at how arid East Timor was generally and this coastal strip in particular, even allowing for the fact that we were visiting during the dry season.

When we arrived at Liquica there was some confusion as to where the UNAMET local headquarters were located. Eventually we were politely pointed in the direction of the Catholic church with its small adjoining compound. There we were briefed on the local security situation by some rugged individuals doing it hard, but not complaining, as they carried out the UNAMET duties at the local level.

Commander Ray Sutton, a New Zealander who was head of the local UNAMET police contingent (CIVPOL), and Captain Justin Roocke, the local UNAMET military liaison officer from Australia, were very direct and to the point. The Liquica district was controlled by supporters of autonomy, those who preferred Indonesian sovereignty, and as a result most independence supporters had fled inland and were unlikely to return to Liquica until voting day. As we sat under the shade of a large tree, which had become an informal meeting point with a temporary table and some planks as benches, we heard that the Timorese resistance had deliberately been less public in Liquica because of militia threats against them. However, there were indications that these independence supporters intended to exercise their right to vote, having already risked their lives to go through the agony of the registration process, which had involved long queues at many locations.

Despite the informality, this briefing was a powerful pointer to the problems that lay ahead for Liquica. Less than five months previously, a massacre had taken place in and around the church and compound where we were talking, with over fifty independence supporters being killed by militia. (An attempt had been made to putty and paint over bullet holes in the church walls.) Then in July, a convoy organised by UNAMET became stranded on the outskirts of Liquica and was attacked by militia from in front and from behind. UNAMET military liaison officers had to work quickly. Lieutenant Colonel Paul Symon, the senior Australian officer working on the ground, at one stage landed on the beach only to be chased by gun-firing militia groups. After considerable manoeuvring, particularly by Captain Roocke who carried no weapons and showed great personal courage in helping to diffuse the situation, the convoy was eventually freed. UNAMET was not going to be cowed by the militia groupings of Liquica, all of whom seemed to have blood on their hands.

We moved off to tour the area and inspected a proposed polling place in a rudimentary set of schoolrooms further west of Liquica towards Balibo. It was at Balibo that five Australian journalists had been killed in 1975 during the Indonesian invasion of East Timor.

It was here that we watched dedicated UN volunteers, including Matthew Aloud, and UNAMET's Assistant Regional Coordinator, Trevor Smith, train electoral officers for the poll to be held, in just three days time. There was nervousness among the local staff, but the general advice was that electoral education had reached most voters through the informal 'bamboo network' in the villages and that following the registration, there was a high level of interest in and understanding of the process.

I tried to focus the discussions on security on polling day. What restrictions were likely to be placed on voters getting to the polling stations? What procedures would be in place to ensure voters' safety? Whilst we were assured that both CIVPOL and the Indonesian police (POLRI) would be providing security and would be present in large numbers, there was real concern that at critical road junctions and other possible control points, militia would make it difficult for voters to reach the booths. This would be especially so in those areas where there were known to be strong pro-independence groupings. Safe passage had to be provided and the best way to do this was to overwhelm the militia with large numbers of CIVPOL and POLRI.

I sensed no tension by this stage of the warm and tranquil afternoon, so wandered over to talk to a number of people who were standing near the convoy. One confident woman told me very firmly that she wanted to vote, was ready to vote, and hoped that the whole business would be dealt with once and for all. I was careful not to ask her which side she was on, but I was surprised by the general goodwill and good humour encountered in an area where the popular consultation would be acutely contested.

Before heading back to Dili, we drove further up into the mountains to another pretty village to review the ballot preparations there. Roadblocks that had been created by militia from time to time were pointed out to us, and I remember thinking how many easy ambush sites existed, especially around the narrow headlands and on steep sections up into the hills and mountains.

We arrived back at the Australian Consulate to swap notes and to be briefed on the events of the day. Returning to the Hotel Turismo late in the afternoon, I discovered that Carlos, my Spanish–Australian acquaintance, was still desperate to get out of Dili. 'Carlos you are still here. What's gone wrong?' I yelled. He replied that arrangements were now complete and he would be flying out the next day. I wished him well and urged him to have a big breakfast or caesar salad for me at one of the Bronte Beach cafes. My mouth watered as he told me he would do so!

Requests from back in Australia to do media spots piled up and I accepted my share of these. This meant a quick trip from the Hotel Turismo along the water-front through parts of central Dili to the Hotel Mahkota. The roof of this rather substantial three-storey building was perfect for the international media who had brought in container loads of equipment for their satellite links back to their home newsrooms. On each visit to the Hotel Mahkota, I climbed several flights of stairs to the rooftop 'studio' to be intercepted by a representative of the ABC, SBS, the BBC or whatever other news organisation wanted an interview. I would then be escorted to a spot on the roof and the camera would roll. The crews cleverly used the various rooftop back-drops, including the main Dili cathedral which was in one direction, the statue of Jesus Christ which was in another direction and the wharf area which was virtually out the front of the hotel.

During these media engagements, I again got to know some outstanding journalists. Vesna Nazor from SBS, and Mark Bowling, Tim Lester and Geoff Thompson from the ABC, were dedicated and determined reporters working in extremely difficult circumstances. Just as committed were some of the back-up crews, such as David 'Batavia' Anderson, a freelance cameraman I had met in Jakarta. I gave him the nickname Batavia because every other night he could be found in key watering holes, even with the bohemian crowd down at Café Batavia, near the port and main railway station in old Jakarta.

The extraordinarily long hours, the tough deadlines, and the ever-present danger these reporters endured would crush the average person. One night I watched a young BBC journalist completely stuff up his 'to camera' wrap-up piece—not once, not twice but three times. He swore vigorously after the third failure, and invited me to take the spot. I remember putting in a subtle jibe during the interview about how people were responding to the pressure of being in East Timor, including those working on the rooftop of the Hotel

Mahkota! The journalist looked at me, cottoned on to my none too subtle dig and actually smiled.

There is no doubt that the media has a very difficult role to play in periods of international crisis. In those crucial days leading up to the ballot and beyond, it had an added role of helping to monitor the conduct of the ballot and in guaranteeing the integrity of the result.

The media helped, by degrees, to stem the tide of violence. However, there were incidents where the militia did not care if they were being filmed or not. I wondered if some of the violence was manufactured for the benefit of the CNN and other cameras. There is no doubt that in Australia some demonstrations are entirely geared for TV coverage.

With one notable exception, I think this was not the case in East Timor. As the media was not acting as an agent provocateur of the violence, I decided to no longer hold back when approached for an interview or for comment. I saw this as being part of the role of an observer delegation and one direct way of reporting back.

When the delegation regrouped late on Friday afternoon, we moved on to a meeting with Lopes Da Cruz, head of the Barisan Rakyat Timor (a pro-autonomy political group) and Indonesia's Ambassador at Large for East Timor. President Habibie had offered the ambassador postings in Europe and elsewhere, but he wanted to stay in East Timor to provide leadership for the BRT. During our discussion, Lopes Da Cruz emphasised that if there was to be an overwhelming vote for independence then the autonomy side would accept the result, which was slightly at odds with what we had been told by others. I reflected on this and concluded that this was code for another eventuality, namely that if the result was close (say 45 per cent for autonomy and 55 per cent for independence), Indonesia would claim that the result was inconclusive, and the status quo would remain.

Lopes Da Cruz was thoughtful and a man of the world. He spoke of the need to promote reconciliation and to avoid a 'winner take all' situation. Autonomy supporters had recently been assured that whatever happened they could remain citizens of Indonesia, so 'Whatever the outcome,' he said, 'East Timor needed a positive relationship with Indonesia in the future'. I quickly interposed that Australia also needed to maintain a proper and positive relationship with Indonesia and this was best based on mutual respect and acknowledgement of our differences.

This was a good note on which to complete our meeting. We took our leave from his picturesque seaside house not far from Dili's wharf area and travelled to the main UNAMET compound to meet with the UN Electoral Commissioners.

The three wise people who had the formal duty of evaluating the integrity of the ballot process had been appointed by the Secretary-General, Kofi Annan, to be independent of UNAMET. Patrick Bradley (from Northern Ireland and therefore, I guess, to some extent used to ballots and bullets) was tall and impressive, a man not to be underestimated. The carefully-spoken and wise South African, Johann Kriegler, had experience of elections in South Africa, including the 1994 election when many people had been killed during a rampage in the central business district of Johannesburg. In complete contrast was Bong Suk Sohn from South Korea, a woman who struck me as being very 'no nonsense' in approach.

The Electoral Commissioners explained that they were examining every aspect of the poll, including its organisation, the political atmosphere in which it was being conducted and the civic education program.

There was good news and bad news. Registration of voters had been an unqualified success, clearly showing the determination of the East Timorese people to qualify for the vote and be part of the process. The security situation, on the other hand, was far from satisfactory, although Patrick Bradley commented that he had been in several countries where poll violence had been far worse, with intimidation being brutally applied.

I was greatly impressed by the three Commissioners and was even starting to get the hang of the UNAMET structure. Separate from the Electoral Commissioners were nine key people who, at various critical stages, risked their lives to provide the discerning leadership necessary to successfully complete the ballot.

Ambassador Jamsheed Marker of Pakistan was the Secretary-General's personal representative. I had met him in Australia whilst I was Acting Prime Minister in July and found him to be a man with a great deal of diplomatic guile and experience. He was responsible for a good deal of the liaison work with governments in the region, but particularly with the Indonesian Government.

The ever cool and prescient Ian Martin from the United Kingdom, created confidence with his personal leadership and quiet demeanour in moments of crisis and chaos. This deeply committed man is a true 'citizen of the world'.

The Chief of the Civilian Police was Commissioner Alan Mills, a retired senior Australian Federal Police officer. Whilst not a tall person, he had a much needed bearing and bluff, which was used on many occasions as the whole of his contingent was unarmed. It is now a matter of public record that this aspect of service in East Timor was considered by Federal Cabinet when I was Deputy Prime Minister and a member of the National Security Committee. There was painstaking

consultation over the issue and only after lengthy deliberation was it decided that CIVPOL and related
personnel should be unarmed. Most of the CIVPOL
personnel I spoke to in East Timor said that this was
the right decision, but what was needed quickly were
separate armed back-up forces.

The Chief Military Liaison Officer, Brigadier General Rezaqul Haider, came from Bangladesh and cut a
dashing figure. His was a very impressive team able to
use maximum leverage through their leadership skills.
Australian Army Lieutenant Colonel Paul Symon, whom
the delegation met in Dili and who I had previously
met in the Middle East, was part of this group.

The Chief Electoral Officer, Jeff Fischer (no relation), was from the USA. Always frank with his answers,
he drove himself to exhaustion. To him must go a great
deal of the credit for conducting a ballot in challenging
conditions, with great rigour and attention to detail.

David Wimhurst, a Canadian, and a superb performer both in Darwin and Dili, was the Chief of Public
Information. His credible performance was in sharp
contrast to the annoying NATO spokesman during the
Kosovo conflict. Getting information to the public was
a very important part of the ballot process, and David
did this well.

I did not meet the other key personnel on the
logistics side, Francesc Vendrell from Spain, Johannes
Wortel of the Netherlands and Beng Yong Chew of
Singapore. However, I have no doubt that along with
all of the others they worked very hard to ensure a
proper ballot. Whatever stuff-ups did occur, the only
ones I encountered were entirely a result of the difficult
security circumstances in East Timor and not the fault
of UNAMET.

At the end of a long second day, we joined the
New Zealand Observer Delegation for a quick bite to

eat at a very small Portuguese restaurant. We swapped notes and agreed on a common assessment of the situation. With two days to go to the ballot, UNAMET had made a Herculean effort to complete all preparations on time. Everything from the actual ballot papers through to the ballot boxes were of a very high standard, and we agreed that prospects were looking good. The New Zealand delegation, led by Roger Maxwell MP, was a good if diverse bunch, who were very committed, dedicated and doing it hard. Phil Gough from the opposition New Zealand Labour Party was delegation deputy leader. Within three months he would become New Zealand's Foreign Minister after the change in government following the November 1999 elections. Such is politics now, more volatility and shorter terms in government.

It already seemed as if I had been in East Timor for two months instead of barely two days. At least, I thought, I was getting to know the Hotel Turismo. I had already surveyed the possible escape routes and hideaway holes in stairwell cavities and the like, just in case a shooting match started in and around the hotel. I was not overly nervous, just being practical in a way I had been trained to be many years before as a junior army officer at the officer training unit Scheyville (OTU) near Windsor west of Sydney.

Exhausted, I called it quits and retired to my room. My final thoughts that night were: a day without violence, and good progress was clearly being made towards the ballot.

FOUR

TO GLENO AND THE HILLS

Saturday 28 August 1999

O UR THIRD DAY began with briefings and another meeting on security. By this stage, the delegation was working very well together. We supported one another and reported back to each other on a raft of individual observations.

The members of the delegation from DFAT were proving to be particularly practical. Stephanie Shwabsky became the scribe, recording the detail for our report back to Alexander Downer. Kirk Conningham and Anthony Pearce performed a hundred and one different roles, coordinating transport within and around Dili, and making arrangements for our various meetings. Occasionally, they were also the court jesters providing much appreciated light relief in the difficult setting, without taking away from their onerous workload.

At first I had struggled with the hot days, but by day three I had become reasonably acclimatised and had adjusted to the two hour time difference. The main build-up to the wet season had not begun and there was little or no wind, so the climate was not unpleasant.

In order to survey conditions away from the coast, it was decided that today the whole delegation would travel inland to the town of Gleno, about 30 kilometres south-west from Dili. The small convoy travelled slowly up a steep winding road crossing over a 800-metre high coastal range to pass through some attractive light rainforest country. In places there were great holes in the road, which would become impassable for long periods during the torrential rain of the wet season.

After climbing over a coastal range, we descended into the Ermera district and then drove up to the town of Gleno, located on a pretty plateau.

Gleno was not unlike Mount Hagen in the PNG Highlands, a small urban area surrounded by a rich fertile mountain plateau bounded by steep mountain ranges. And like Mount Hagen, coffee plantations were a feature of the area. Quite profitable in a good season, the coffee produced around Gleno was chemical free, so it had the potential to be marketed as 'boutique' or organic coffee. Nevertheless, agricultural development was very limited, with a form of simple cottage farming dominating. Sadly, even in a good year with a good wet season, the fertile plateau of Ermera was unable to produce enough rice to feed the district. Some 400 tonnes of rice a month had to be shipped in. I made a note to myself that aid programs to East Timor should relate to agriculture development and provide improved varieties to expand coffee and rice production.

Gleno was a relatively new district capital built by Indonesia, guessing by the style of the buildings, which were mainly single storey. We drove through the town and turned up a back street passing modest housing. Made of concrete blocks with galvanised-iron roofs, many of the houses also had satellite dishes.

The convoy arrived at the local UNAMET head-quarters to be met by a big-hearted Australian, Superintendent Geoffrey Hazel, the local CIVPOL leader. Geoffrey Hazel, who stood tall and proud in his uniform, was from Canberra and had volunteered for this tour of duty, a long way from armed back-up. He explained how his team had established a policy of active patrolling, despite the difficulties created by the rugged terrain beyond the plateau and the continuing intimidation by members of the local pro-autonomy militia.

There was plenty of evidence that large numbers of hardcore militia were established in and around Gleno. The activities of a TNI detachment, who were supplying ammunition to the militia, were of particular concern as were the Indonesian police, who had not made a single arrest despite clearly illegal militia activities.

Diane Baker and Helene Van Klinken, both UNAMET staff, also briefed the delegation and reported that good progress had been made with electoral education and ballot preparations. They were very confident that the population of Ermera knew how to indicate their choice on the ballot paper—either by marking with a sign or by punching a hole (both were allow-able)—but were concerned about security.

A group from the delegation, led by Laurie Brereton, made a side visit to a large Falintil cantonment in the hills about an hour's drive from Gleno. Way back in September 1974, before the Portuguese had formally departed, Fretilin formed its military arm, known as Falintil, to push forward a guerilla war for the independence of East Timor. Falintil forces were relatively small but were well-disciplined and said to be well-trained and well-led by Field Commander Tauar Matan Ruak. These forces were ranged against not just the TNI, but also against the pro-Indonesian militia. One estimate put the number of

Falintil supporters in the Ermera district at over ten thousand. The local commander, Ular, confirmed that all his troops were registered to vote, and would attend the polling places on Monday in civilian clothing. The delegation returned from the hills excited by their warm reception and upbeat about the commitment of this group of East Timorese to the ballot. They seemed happy enough with the security at the cantonment which had over recent months become a Falintil safe haven.

Ambassador John McCarthy and I headed off to meet the *Bupati* (Indonesian-appointed District Governor), Dr Constantino Soares, first at his office and then at his house, in a superb location on top of a small hill overlooking the plateau. Both at the formal meeting in his downtown office and over a delicious buffet lunch at his home, it was apparent that Dr Soares enjoyed very good relations with the UNAMET officers, who had obviously worked hard to bring about this meeting.

Dr Soares expected a peaceful polling day throughout his district and was planning to distribute rations to internally displaced people (IDPs), those who had fled their homes through fear of intimidation and violence in the build-up to the poll, to help ease food shortages. I wondered how close Dr Soares was to the Indonesian Army, and to what extent he would be given a free hand in nursing his district through the poll and its aftermath. While I was careful not to ask him about his own voting intentions, I got the impression that he was leaning towards pro-autonomy and the maintenance of Indonesian sovereignty. However, he did refer to an uncle, a local priest, who was an activist with the independence movement. (This was confirmed by several sources.)

At the end of the very pleasant lunch, I sincerely thanked Constantino Soares and his team and family for their very generous hospitality. I also reminded him that for a period the Australian Government had been in favour of special autonomy for East Timor with continuing Indonesian sovereignty. However, we now recognised that this was a matter for choice by the East Timorese people. Australia had nothing to gain by the break up of Indonesia and wanted to see continued good relations, but the East Timor question needed to be resolved. We would accept the result of the poll, whatever it might be.

Over the years I have become a student of the use of body language in trade negotiations and politics generally. I thought Dr Soares was not lying and that he was trying harder to keep the peace than any of the other *bupatis* we were to meet.

Returning to the UNAMET headquarters at Gleno, we met up with an NGO observer delegation from ANFREL, a Bangkok-based justice organisation. These dedicated citizens of the world were of all ages and included everybody from so-called 'bleeding heart liberals' to wise and more experienced observers. I was deeply impressed by their commitment, and their personal generosity. Many of the volunteer observers met their own costs, which sometimes made me feel slightly less than pure as an observer as here I was in East Timor at the Australian Government's expense.

There was no doubt that enormous effort had gone into the preparations for the poll in Gleno and its environs. Many difficulties had to be overcome. Local communications were next to zero even though telephone or mobilenet links existed, although mainly for the area around Dili. In our discussions in Gleno, UNAMET made it very clear that the most important thing observer delegations could do on polling day was to be highly visible, particularly along roads and at congregation points leading to polling sites. The aim was to have the eyes of the world focused on East Timor so that the militia would behave and scale back atrocities during this period. I thought this made a lot of sense and it would allow us, in turn, to report on the extent of free access to polling places.

The convoy eventually headed back to Dili, past a couple of polling places in Gleno, and across the one key bridge on the main road.

As we drove along the Dili waterfront, I noticed that the regular Indonesian ferry was alongside and being loaded with what looked like boxes of household belongings. The ferry was painted attractively in gold and white and was about the same size as the ferries that travel across the Bass Strait to Tasmania and between the north and south islands of New Zealand.

Already some of the Indonesian elite were pulling out, not even waiting to see which way the ballot would go. The ferry was a safe way to remove belongings and to transfer to various parts of Indonesia. I watched a four-wheel drive vehicle pull in to the wharf loaded with household items such as TV sets and refrigerators. For one group the big move was well and truly on.

Some of the Indonesians who moved to East Timor in the late seventies and the early eighties believed that Jakarta's U-turn in allowing a ballot was a bitter pill, if not an outright betrayal. After years of making money and lording it over the local population, their livelihoods and their homes were now in jeopardy. Those who thought there would be a big pro-independence vote were leaving early, but perhaps they also knew of plans to destroy East Timor after the ballot outcome was announced and wanted to be well clear of the area.

A small Indonesian patrol boat was at anchor just out to sea, keeping a baleful eye on proceedings along the Dili foreshore. One or two patrol boats cruising along the coast near Dili were not going to have much of an impact. However, there were rumours of night-time activity on isolated beaches, with the Indonesian Navy supplying militia units. It was difficult keeping track of the allegations, and it was not the delegation's job to do so, but I was confident that a good deal of satellite and other monitoring was occurring.

Back at the Hotel Turismo we had a 30-minute break before the next round of meetings. I thought a quick shower would be great. Alas, the lock to my room jammed and my key was completely useless even though it slipped easily in and out. In total frustration I nearly kicked the door, but restrained myself enough to go back to the front desk to ask for help. To my total surprise within five minutes the lock had been changed, new keys issued and I was under the shower getting ready for the meetings ahead. Full thanks to the hotel's hardworking staff.

Our next appointment was with the man who had shared his Nobel Peace prize with the people of East Timor, Bishop Carlos Filipe Ximenes Belo. His residence in Dili was conveniently alongside the Hotel Turismo. The Bishop was right on time and, smiling as always, he ushered us in to his small lounge. He seemed tired and tense—understandably so. The Bishop was very forthcoming on a range of issues.

In this 90 per cent Catholic country, Bishop Belo said the Church did not support one side or another in East Timor. There were Catholics on both sides. The Church had a significant role in the reconciliation process and in a recent pastoral letter, he had explained the background of the Act of Consultation and urged the East Timorese people to go to the polls and vote according to their conscience.

The Bishop's comments on the difficulties that would exist after the result was announced proved prescient. If the vote were to be for staying with Indonesia, the pro-independence guerillas would fight on. If the vote was for independence, the militias would take to the streets. But I took particular note of his plea that an international force—and an armed force at that—would be needed after a pro-independence vote. While consideration of this issue was technically outside the brief of the Australian Observer Delegation, Laurie Brereton continued to push the Bishop on the need for an armed peace-making/peace-keeping force. Bishop Belo's comments were relayed to Alexander Downer in the delegations official report which was handed to the Minister on Friday 3 September, six days after the meeting took place.

> The Bishop stated that he believed many East Timorese had not registered to vote because of intimidation and fears about security. He indicated that the supporters of autonomy had manipulated the security situation and that the police were unable and unwilling to control the activities of the militias. The Bishop considered that the pro-independence fighters were unlikely to accept a pro-autonomy result and the war in East Timor would continue. If the independence side won there would be seven or eight days of violence and then the militias would give up. He considered that East Timor would need an international force to keep order and that it was impossible to rely on the Indonesian forces to keep order in the interim period until the People's Consultative Assembly or MPR made its decision on East Timor.

There is no doubt that the Catholic Church was very active at various stages in the process that led to the ballot. Some members of the Church actively promoted independence, others (probably the majority) were concerned to ensure that the ballot was free and fair. It was instructive that Bishop Belo, particularly in his pastoral letter, was careful in urging people to vote according to their conscience. He was convincing on that point, but the message was less clear when we discussed how much he knew of pro-independence activity by parish priests.

After a group photo on the steps of Bishop Belo's residence, we moved on to the UNAMET compound. The delegation, through the good work of Consul James Batley and others, was being given high priority with appointments. To my amazement, we sat down in a conference hall at UNAMET with the 'big four'. Ian Martin, Head of UNAMET was looking as cool and as calm as always. Next to him sat Jeff Fischer, UNAMET Chief Electoral Officer, who would shortly be joined by the Chief of the Civilian Police, Commissioner Alan Mills, and the Chief Military Liaison Officer, Brigadier General Rezaqul Haider. It might have helped that Ingrid Hayden, the daughter of former Australian Governor-General Bill Hayden was the secretary and a personal assistant to Ian Martin, but given the many delegations in town and the fact the poll was less than 36 hours away, I greatly appreciated the time and high-level access we were granted.

The 'big four' had succeeded, against all odds, in bringing the ballot to this stage of preparation. The fact that over 450 000 East Timorese had registered to vote was a great credit to them and their respective teams. Ian Martin was upbeat; he pointed out that the Indonesian Government had recently changed some of the more difficult military commanders in East Timor. At the same time, pressure from Australia and elsewhere had brought about an improvement in the level of cooperation (and not just the rhetoric) with both the Indonesian Army and the Indonesian Police Force. Tomorrow morning Ian Martin announced, on the eve of the ballot, a major press conference would take place involving leaders of the militia, Falintil and the CNRT where, he hoped, they would shake hands and publicly declare their support for a new agreement banning the carriage of weapons in public areas.

Keeping in mind that there could still be massive last-minute hitches, Ian Martin explained that the poll would proceed on time, but a low voter turn out would mean that UNAMET had failed to provide protection and security. Once again, we were urged to cover as much ground as possible on polling day as this would undoubtedly assist the process, especially in establishing the integrity of the ballot.

We wished everyone good luck and left the UNAMET compound for a beachside fish restaurant located in a tin shed between the Hotel Turismo and the statue of Jesus Christ. The fish was truly excellent, the tin shed truly awful. As we ate, I realised how vulnerable we were to stoning and gunfire, but gathered that our security detail had negotiated with the local militia to ensure we had a peaceful dinner. We swapped notes and observations and updated one another before heading back to the Hotel Turismo to ring home and get ready for an early start the next day.

After all the activity of each day, I had no trouble in plunging into a deep sleep. At the same time I had hoped I would lose a bit of weight in East Timor, but alas this had not occurred so far.

FIVE

POLLING DAY EVE

Sunday 29 August 1999

IT WAS A case of being up early again to walk next door to attend 6 am Mass in the garden of Bishop Belo's residence. During our meeting with the Bishop the previous evening we asked if we could join the service. He said that all would be welcome and implied that he would be saying Mass.

I guess there must have been close to a thousand people in front of a simple altar under a wooden pergola. The Bishop's chooks cackled away nearby. Some five television camera crews also turned up and plonked in the middle of the worshippers. Most delegation members moved over to one side, against a small wall, so as not to impose on or block the view of the congregation. The East Timorese, who were there to worship, had reason not to be impressed by the large intrusion from outside.

Justice John Dowd from Amnesty International came up and said hello. We were both in the New South Wales Parliament together and he was for a period New

South Wales Attorney-General. Now he was very keen to see the ballot succeed.

The congregation comprised all age groups and included large numbers of young people. As is often the case when the Church is under threat, there was a strong and obvious display of devotion. This was in sharp contrast to the more casual commitment shown at the church gatherings I frequent in the Riverina and north-east Victoria areas of Australia.

To our surprise a young priest, and not Bishop Belo, joined the precession behind about ten altar boys and assistants. We learnt later that the Bishop had travelled down to Suai near the West Timor border, despite the difficult security conditions, to encourage the people in that hotspot to vote. During our meeting, Bishop Belo had not mentioned that he would be making this difficult trip. Perhaps he had not yet decided to go, or maybe it was a matter of security: the need to keep his movements under wraps was obvious enough. Notwithstanding his absence, the Mass was invigorating and fortifying, adding a degree of comfort to the final build-up to the poll the next day.

After Mass, I returned to the Hotel Turismo and was told Carlos had gone. I thought, 'damn it, he's probably having that big breakfast or a caesar salad at Bronte Beach. Half his luck.' He wrote to me later:

This is just to express my appreciation for your help
and attention whilst in East Timor some three weeks
ago. As you might remember the Hotel Dili, where I
was staying, was attacked by the militias on the
afternoon of Thursday 26 August. For around 20
minutes I really thought they were going to kill all of
us. It was really scary. Three hours after the attack we
were evacuated by the Indonesian police to Hotel
Turismo, where you were staying with the Australian

Parliamentary Observer Mission. I was quite agitated
and distressed at that time, and I just wanted to thank
you for your understanding and the help you gave that
night in calming me down and the following day
when I was trying to find the first plane out of Dili.

Please accept my heartfelt gratitude and if either
myself or my agency can be of any future assistance to
you, please do not hesitate to contact me.

Coincidently, as one reporter departed another
arrived. Sarah Boyd, a young and attractive New Zealand journalist from NZBC, seemed to have been
thrown in the deep end, and at short notice. I gave her
some hints about the key contacts around Dili and a
couple of interviews for NZBC, and urged her to keep
her head down.

Lieutenant Colonel Paul Symon and I then sat down
to enjoy our one-egg breakfast feast. It is always good
to be able to speak directly to people 'on the front line',
as you learn so much. I did this regularly as part of a
two-pronged strategy when I was Minister for Trade.
The first part of the strategy was to do one work-related
activity a month that was my personal choice and that
reflected my priorities (as opposed to the 1001 commitments made on my behalf that reflected everybody else's
priorities). For the second stage, from time to time I
would meet with all officers, from the most senior to
the most junior, in a particular section of the Department of Foreign Affairs and Trade for their direct views
on any number of issues. For example, I would ask to
speak to all of the officers on the Thailand desk and
probe them about the economic trends in Thailand and
its ASEAN role.

Here in Dili, my strategy was to 'pick the brains'
of an army colonel I had first met in the Middle East,
where he was carrying out dangerous UN peace-keeping

work. Paul Symon had acquitted himself well in difficult UN operations in Israel and Lebanon and I guess this was why he was suddenly selected to take up a senior staff officer position with UNAMET. He had just five days notice to pack and say goodbye to his young family before first going to New York and then to Dili. He had been on the ground in Dili for some two months in the lead up to the ballot and was obviously building good networks, helped no doubt by the fact that he and Colonel Muis had attended Australian Army Staff College together.

Over breakfast I learnt of the great difficulties UNAMET faced during the early weeks, difficulties that forced a delay in the registration process and then a delay in setting a date for the ballot. (In July, the militia mounted a number of attacks on registration centres during which one East Timorese was killed and several others injured.) Both CIVPOL, who were in the vanguard, and the military liaison people had to draw on real leadership skills. This was especially true in places like Liquica, Suai and Maliana where direct threats were being made by local pro-autonomy militias.

Thinking that Paul Symon would be great on radio as a direct voice from Timor, I had the idea of trying to get a slot on the ABC's 'Australia All Over'. This incredibly popular program is taken by 57 ABC radio stations right across Australia, both metropolitan and rural. Its compere, the extraordinary Ian McNamara, could probably be described as the most dedicated but also most disorganised and democratic radio anchorman in Australia, and he is free of any cash for comment sagas. Over my 30 years in active politics, I have always given absolute priority to ABC Radio because of its widespread coverage across country Australia and, in turn, supported it in Budget deliberations, I had come to know Ian well. In some ways, his program represents the best and most positive in Australian society. At other times, it can be very negative, pushing the mantra of no change. When on working trips overseas, I sometimes arranged for lively Aussie exporters to ring in as a way of breaking down some of the insularity that exists in the rural and manufacturing industries.

I eventually got through to the program producer, but they were pretty loaded up and had already taken a call from East Timor that morning, so we missed out on Macca. To spread this on-the-ground reporting around, I switched my energies to getting Paul some live interviews on commercial radio stations. He was particularly good in an interview with a Brisbane station, which was a foretaste of what senior military personnel would soon be doing every day of the week from Dili.

Paul's brother Craig had been my Chief-of-Staff up until late 1998. He had given me a parcel of goodies, including some *Bulletin's*, to bring up to Paul and I was happy to help at least one person assuage some homesickness.

After breakfast I joined the Ambassador at the UNAMET headquarters for the now infamous press conference. There were no less than 22 television cameras waiting as Ian Martin brought together in one room the leaders of the pro-autonomy groups and the leaders of the pro-independence groups. There was real tension in the air as it was announced that an agreement had been reached between both sides. They would cooperate with UNAMET on polling day and beyond by banning the carrying of arms in public places. I wondered how long this form of cease-fire would last as I watched the leaders embrace one another in scenes reminiscent of Fidel Castro's appearance at the WTO summit in Geneva in May of 1998. On that bizarre occasion a long queue of dark-suited diplomats, who had no doubt been wild student radicals in the sixties, waited in line to embrace Castro. Hypocrites I thought, as most of those bear-hugging delegates came from WTO countries where elections are held that can change governments, unlike in Castro's Cuba. (I noticed that Fidel Castro was smart enough to stay away from the WTO Seattle debacle held in December 1999 and now known as the Battle of Seattle.)

Despite my concern about the future of the agreement, the press conference went very well. Good spirits, even friendship, hung in the air. For the first time I sensed a growing spirit of excitement amongst all present as I saw a smiling Eurico Guterres, from the dangerous Aitarak militia based in Dili, bear hug the Falintil Field Commander Tauar Matan Ruak. Eurico had long hair and a fresh countenance that made him look almost innocent, whereas Tauar looked sinister and fierce. Given the record of the militia up until then, this was a case of 'looks can be deceiving'.

At the end of the press conference, I was briefed as leader of the delegation on conduct for the observer delegations during polling day. The guidelines represented commonsense. For example, observers could not stand behind voters as they marked their ballot papers and, importantly, you could not ask voters how they proposed to vote. An attempt was also made to spread observer delegations so that there wouldn't be massive duplication in some areas and no representatives in others. Some of the Australian delegation would be going to Maliana near the West Timor border. As there were big security and logistical issues to be resolved, I decided to raise this matter further at a delegation meeting that afternoon.

It soon became obvious that we were going to have people on the ground for the length and breadth of East Timor. Like me and many other international observers, two Chilean parliamentary observers at the briefing, Juan Pablo Leteher and Ignasio Walker, were keen and excited about the poll, but also concerned about its aftermath. In all, there were probably over 100 observers at the meeting representing over 50 separate delegations.

I rejoined the Australian delegation, which was once again to be split into two to cover more ground. One group would be going east of Dili to Manatuto and the other due south, to Aileu.

I was going east for the first time, on a road that led to the Jesus Christ statue and went past some very big road slippages (the word crater came to mind as I viewed the supersized potholes that vehicles had to narrowly squeeze past). This section of the coastline was quite attractive and was dominated by banana and coconut plantations. There were very few houses or buildings to be seen and there was very little activity. The big tourist resorts that you would expect to find along pretty coastlines, such as in Bali, were totally absent. In the future, there will undoubtedly be some tourist resort development, but hopefully developers will learn from the mistakes made in Australia and throughout Asia so that the resorts blend with the local environment, rather than clash with it.

It was late morning, and hot and dusty when we arrived at Manatuto, a coastal town and capital of the Polres Manatuto District. We found the local UNAMET electoral officer, Martin Landy, and the military liaison officer, Major John Petrie, in their headquarters, a tiny house in a back street. They gave the delegation an excellent briefing, expressing concern about the local district governor (*bupati*) and his connection with militia activity in the area. The *bupati*, who is effectively appointed by the Indonesian authorities, has a good deal of control over the district. We were also advised that many independence supporters had fled into the hills after registration but were committed to return to vote the next day. Preparation, particularly the distribution of polling place material, seemed to be right on schedule, a credit again to the professionalism of the UNAMET officers.

Just as we were about to depart the UNAMET headquarters, two truckloads of East Timorese pulled up to say that they had heard rumours of roadblocks between Dili and Manatuto. They were particularly concerned as they were on their way to vote in Dili, where they had registered to avoid persecution in their village further east. We were able to inform them that there were absolutely no roadblocks between Dili and Manatuto and that later in the afternoon we would be travelling back along the road in convoy with a small security detail. This seemed to please them and they jumped back into their trucks and headed off towards Dili. This incident confirmed to me the absolute determination of the East Timorese to vote, even if it meant travelling long distances in difficult circumstances. I stood in awe of these people, jammed tightly in the back of open trucks. They displayed true commitment to the vote and the right to make a fundamental choice about their futures.

The delegation then went on to meet the *bupati*, one of the key district governors in East Timor, in his well protected hillside residence in Manatuto. While it was established protocol that visiting international delegations call on the local *bupati*, we also saw it as a real opportunity to get a handle on control on the ground and who the local government was backing. This *bupati* was not without considerable wealth and connections having been a trucking contractor, his contract work for the Indonesians covering a large part of East Timor. On the top shelf of a cabinet in his lounge room were not one, but two giant bottles of whisky, Chivas Regal and Johnny Walker Black Label at that, curiously gathering dust.

We learnt from the *bupati* that he had a second residence in Bali and that he had much to lose from independence as Indonesian patronage would be lost and his commercial operations would be affected.

On this occasion the assurances we sought and obtained were less believable. I was very uncomfortable as this meeting dragged on. The only real information we took when we left was that some of the pro-Indonesian groups obviously thought they still had a chance of obtaining between 45 per cent to 50 per cent of the vote. And thank God they did.

This explained why the final preparations for the poll were continuing with some resistance, but with no outright blockage. As the pro-Indonesian elements were not anticipating a huge turnout, they thought they were 'in with a chance', or at least close enough to argue that the status quo should be maintained. It was just as well that they believed this, as it meant that militia activity was reduced a little during this critical period.

There was no doubt in my mind that the militia hated President Habibie's undertaking to hold a ballot in East Timor. They regarded Jakarta's decision as an outright betrayal. There was also no doubt in my mind that the militia had the ability to shut down the whole process leading to the poll at any time they chose.

The militia were well armed and had a command structure that enabled them to turn on and turn off violence at their will. Whenever General Wiranto visited Dili, militia activity would immediately quieten down. The militia were the wild card on the ground, ready to slaughter voters with a simple change of mind, but what would they do in the last days leading up to the poll? I concluded their tactics were an evil two-dimensional mixture.

First, they threatened the East Timorese, especially where independence support was strong. These threats were designed to either scare locals from fronting up to vote or to make them think twice about voting for independence because of the murder and mayhem that was sure to follow. Second, they refrained from shooting UN staff and international observers, at least prior to the ballot day. This meant that we felt a degree of safety even though there were plenty of opportunities for ambush and kidnap. I did not feel in acute personal danger at any stage, but then again we had the protection of the Australian Federal Police contingent and the Indonesian police detail under the command of the ever-smiling Lieutenant Arly.

After our meeting with the *bupati*, we went down to a local church and walked along the solid stone seawall of a nearby beach. Here we watched young children dance between the splashing of the waves. Their simple fun and cheerful laughter were a tonic to the team.

During our visit to Manatuto we also met Father Peter Hosking SJ, a young parish priest from Richmond in Victoria, who had somehow secured himself leave to take up a counselling job with UNAMET. I joked that there would have to be a Jesuit or two somewhere in the plot. Peter laughed and explained that his work involved a lot of trauma counselling, the aftermath of militia activity. Not only had this killing and deliberate destruction of towns and villages traumatised the East Timorese, UNAMET personnel were also affected.

Years ago I received a Jesuit education at Xavier College in Melbourne. This gave me a flying start in working out where Peter was coming from and here I found a Jesuit who was a very dedicated, articulate and intelligent counsellor. And like most Jesuits he would rather be on the move, so I understood his frustration at being penned in at headquarters in Dili. He very much preferred getting out and about to observe conditions first-hand and work with staff in the field.

Back in Dili, the delegation met in the upstairs conference room of the Hotel Turismo to discuss the security risks for polling day. Federal Police officers Paul Cartwright and Craig Jacobsen had travelled with us from Canberra. They were in their mid-thirties and fit and friendly, and like everyone else were unarmed. I thought it would be hypocritical in the extreme if they were allowed to have personal weapons when their colleagues in CIVPOL and the military liaison officers weren't. I checked this detail before leaving Canberra and had been assured by the East Timor DFAT task force leader, Chris Moraitis, that neither would be carrying weapons.

Paul and Craig had made inquiries and an assessment on the safety of going to Balibo and Maliana in the dark, very early on polling morning. There was a real concern about safety and security on the long and winding road to Maliano through Liquica. The Ambassador, John McCarthy, became involved and eventually it was decided the risk involved was not too great. I prayed this would be the case, as I did not want to lose any of the delegation. Paul and Craig gently reminded me not to take their role for granted and explained to everyone that the security situation was still volatile, indeed, very risky. I thought I was being chastised in a not too gentle way and I accepted the hint being dropped. I resolved to be more cautious personally, as well as to be polite and pleasant to all the security officers as sometimes I would take short cuts past them.

The problem was my longstanding desire for personal space. I recall at one conference in Africa I became so weary of having security personnel watch my every move that I grabbed the sleeve microphone of my assigned South African agent and yelled into it, 'Minister out of control'. I was walking backwards to an escalator and added down the microphone, 'Do not panic as we should be able to get situation back under control!'. By the time we arrived at the bottom, a small group of perplexed senior agents were waiting. I gave them all a big smile and moved on into the conference room. I took the view that if I was going to be branded by the media as being idiosyncratic, I might as well live up to the reputation!

The delegation would be split into two for polling day, so it was agreed that those going to Balibo and Maliana near the West Timor border would rise at 2.30 am for a 3 am departure. This group would include both Marise Payne and Laurie Brereton. I suggested they should get an early night and absolved them from attending a dinner with the European Union Official Observer Delegation. I wished them well and knew I did not have to remind them of what happened in Balibo 24 years ago. The second group was to be on deck by 5.45 am and ready to roll for a long day in Dili.

Before going downstairs for dinner with the Europeans, we all met with CNRT leaders, Leandro Isaacs and David Ximenes. They were very tense as there had been further incidents around Dili that afternoon, notwithstanding the earlier 'no firearms' agreement. The CNRT was Falintil's peak organisation and its leaders told us of many accounts of harassment by the militia. They expressed real concerns about what might happen on polling day. Leandro Isaacs and David Ximenes were not in any way arrogant or bombastic, indeed, they were softly spoken and obviously bone-weary given all that they had been through. They told us they had become used to the subterfuge needed to disguise their movements around Dili and beyond. They spoke of their fears of being stalked, but also expressed hope that their people would seize this opportunity and step forward and vote.

The European Union Observer Delegation was led by Irish Foreign Minister, David Andrews. Just for once I refrained from making a major attack on the European common agricultural policy, restricting myself to one brief outburst. The focus of our discussions was on the Indonesian reaction to a strong vote for independence.

I recalled a discussion I had had with Ali Alatas on the margins of the first meeting of the Indian Ocean Rim Association for Regional Cooperation (IORARC). This was held in Mauritius in 1997 in an isolated conference centre that had just one photocopier. The conference officials were trying to run off the final communiqué on this overloaded machine. As luck would have it, the breakdown of the photocopier led to the conference being suspended for one hour giving delegates the opportunity to stroll with one another and engage in unscripted conversation, without note-takers present. Suddenly I found myself in a relaxed conversation with Ali Alatas on a range of issues including, briefly, East Timor. He expressed weariness over the East Timor issue and suggested that once the 'old man', by this he meant President Soeharto, moved on from the presidency there would be real movement by Indonesia to resolve the long-running issue. In short, Ali Alatas described East Timor as a time-consuming distraction devouring enormous resources, and a problem that had to be solved, although he did not detail any options or solutions.

Just one year later, Soeharto, who had provided strong economic leadership and given Indonesia considerable stability, was gone. Another year on, Indonesia had proposed the ballot on the future of East Timor. So, Ali Alatas was correct with his informal prediction, but he was also under enormous pressure from the military faction in the Indonesian Government, which was determined to hold on to East Timor at all costs.

I also recounted how, on my last two key visits to Jakarta, I made the mistake of over-praising President Soeharto's economic leadership, but I have always had the view that Australia was better off with a cohesive, economically strong Indonesia rather than an economic sinkhole to our north. After the rip and tear of the bilateral relationship between Australia and Indonesia over East Timor, I submitted that in the new century trade would recover quickly. Diplomatic warmth, however, would take longer to return.

Our European friends believed that the TNI and Indonesia would have to accept the outcome of the ballot, but only after a period of militia-provoked anger. With this thought we wished one another luck and went to bed with a prayer that all would go well on polling day.

SIX

THE BIG DAY AT LAST

Monday 30 August 1999

POLLING DAY HAD finally arrived. Dawn brought a few clouds and a tinge of pink on the horizon. There was a buzz of excitement around the hotel courtyard. Even Bishop Belo's chooks could be heard cackling away more loudly than usual. The extra traffic and movement of people had obviously set them off. The Maliana group had departed on time at around 3 am, and we were now ready to go full swing into the busiest day of the visit, to observe all aspects of the ballot. I completed a number of interviews back to Australia before we had a quick snack and jumped into the vehicles to inspect our designated polling places.

Our first port of call was polling place number 21 in Dili East, the Bidau Santana Primary School located up a narrow road about two kilometres from the Hotel Turismo. There I noticed not ten or twenty people, but hundreds making their way to the school. The militia had put away their guns and knives, the Falintil had done likewise, and it was a case of everyone heading to the polling place where they had registered a few weeks before. There was real excitement in the air as people, who seemed to be dressed in their Sunday best, held up their registration cards and moved quietly towards the entrance gates. Many TV crews were also present and not causing any difficulties.

Vicki Bourne and I worked our way through the crowd to get to the iron-grille gates as we needed to be inside before 6.30 am. Our job was to inspect and sign off that all ballot boxes were empty. We squeezed through the gates, which were held open just wide enough to allow the observers into the polling compound where we met the officials who showed us the preparations they had made. We inspected each of the ballot boxes, which were of durable plastic, coloured blue and grey. They were cleverly designed to incorporate seals to ensure the lid could not be removed. Any tampering would be obvious.

By 6.30 am, the official start time, the clearly very happy and very excited crowd had swelled. The gates opened to a rush of East Timorese voters who, once inside, formed into queues in front of electoral officials sitting at tables. I could not believe the commitment and the absolute joy on so many faces as people proudly held up their registration cards and their identity papers.

After a slow start, as locally trained staff got used to the procedures, the voting commenced. This was it I thought. Those brave people who a month ago had stepped forward and registered were now back in their thousands to vote, to express their free choice on the future of their country.

Each voter approached a table, was identified and had his or her name crossed off the electoral roll. Voters' fingers were checked using a special light machine to see if they had previously voted and invisible ink was then placed on their fingers to ensure they did not vote a second time elsewhere. The ballot paper was then handed to the voter who was invited to go behind a cardboard screen to cast their vote in absolute privacy (very much as occurs in Australia). These mobile screens folded out and a small bench was formed from what looked like a cardboard box. The only difficulty was that some voters thought they should put their ballot paper inside the booth rather than walk back to the official blue ballot box, but they were soon guided in the right direction. I completed the check forms with a whole lot of questions about procedures: Did the polling place open on time? Had the ballot boxes been inspected? Everything was happening in a most orderly manner.

I surveyed the crowd as we prepared to move on to the next polling place. The polite determination of the East Timorese was something to behold, as was their good humour and patience as they stood for long periods waiting to vote. After nearly a quarter of a century, and against all odds, their moment had arrived. Vicki Bourne was so overwhelmed that she did what we all wanted to do at various times throughout the day, she burst into tears. Vicki subsequently told me that she would do this a total of four times during that extraordinary day. The scene at polling place number 21 was very emotional, very exciting and was replicated at many other polling places across East Timor during the day.

The delegation moved on to visit another three polling stations in Dili, Station 007 in Colmera, 009 in Fatuhada, and 029 in Lahane Timur. Despite the huge crowds and long queues at all of these polling places during the first few hours of voting, electoral staff were coping well.

Meanwhile the Australian media were telephoning

every few minutes so I shared around some of the requests for interviews. Stephanie Shwabsky did an interview with SkyTV, which was, I think, probably the first direct interview this dedicated DFAT officer had ever given. We lightened up the occasion by reminding her that she was now, in effect, talking to every pub and club in Australia. Despite our heckling, Stephanie's interview was very successful even though it occurred in a surreal setting alongside two tennis courts that were part of the college campus where polling place 007 was located in downtown Dili. Young kids played tennis while their parents waited to vote in a scene that was entirely happy, peaceful, and beyond all expectations.

I phoned Alexander Downer who was preparing for Question Time after the Monday morning Cabinet meeting and told him that the poll was off to a flying start. Procedures had, by and large, been peacefully complied with. He was greatly pleased by this informal report and said that he would go into Question Time and relay this update directly to the House of Representatives at noon, East Timor time. I told Alexander that he owed me a beer, and I added that I would consider any offers to join future observer missions very carefully. I vividly recall Alexander responding that the opportunity to observe the possible birth of a new nation was a real privilege. On that note the mobile phone dropped out, which might have been just as well, as events turned out.

As we were refuelling at the only petrol station I had seen in East Timor, Alexander Downer was reporting to the House of Representatives.

As members of the House will know, today is indeed an historic day. Today is the day when the people of East Timor, after a quarter of a century of strife, have the opportunity to express their own views about the future of East Timor. We hope that the day will proceed smoothly and that the great problem of East Timor will finally be resolved through these democratic means.

The polling stations opened this morning at 6.30 Dili time—that is, 8.30 Canberra time—across East Timor, so they have now been open for around six hours. The preliminary reports I have received, including a telephone conversation just before question time with Tim Fischer, the leader of the Australian delegation, have been encouraging—that, overall, the situation in East Timor is relatively calm. Apparently voters lined up this morning in great numbers, well before the polling booths opened, to cast their votes. There has been little sign so far of violence or intimidation, particularly in trouble spots such as Maliana. Mr Fischer told me that the voting procedures are operating very smoothly. Clearly, in terms of assessing the fairness of the ballot, the nature of the procedures is a very important component of that.

The government warmly applauds the determination and the resilience of the United Nations on the ground in East Timor for bringing this ballot to fruition. I would single out two people—the leader of UNAMET, Mr Ian Martin, who has done an outstanding job, and the leader of the United Nations civilian police operation, our own Alan Mills, who has won the respect and admiration of all who have dealt with him in East Timor. He is one of many Australians who can be very proud of the role they have played in bringing this ballot about. We should also think of the large number of Australians who are involved in UNAMET—107 or 108 Australians are involved in UNAMET—and who have worked in very difficult circumstances. They have worked tirelessly to try to help the people of East Timor find themselves in the situation they are in today, able to determine their own future.

This is an issue of very great importance to Australia and it is an issue of considerable importance to our part of the world. It will mean a great deal to us if it is resolved in a satisfactory and democratic way. Today is indeed a very historic day and we hope that, by the end of the day, the people of East Timor will have been able to express their views about their future. We will not know what their views are for quite some time as it is our expectation that the results of the ballot will not be announced until around 7 September.

It was now around 11 am. The day had become much warmer as we prepared to move from Dili to Liquica. A '60 Minutes' team from Australia, led by Richard Carleton, had arranged to follow us and did so in a hired red taxi. I had no objection to them coming along as there were media filming the vote all over East Timor.

We arrived at polling station 42/43 in Liquica at around 11.40 in the morning. The scene was peaceful, and the queues at this polling station, located in modest school buildings set in pretty bushland about a kilometre from a nearby beach, were smaller than we'd observed in Dili. In the background, we could see militia standing in their red berets. I made a note of this as we moved forward to carry out our official observations one more time.

The electoral staff requested that there be no filming inside the polling place. Just outside the school buildings, I had an informal interview with Richard Carleton about the process and I told him that we would be moving on to the next polling place in downtown Liquica. As we were about to depart, I noticed that he was asking questions of voters in one of the queues. (I learnt later that these were direct questions about whether they were going to vote for independence or for autonomy.) This attracted the attention of a militia leader who moved over to closely observe the proceedings. I recall that at this stage Richard Carleton was actually inside a taped-off area, which had been put in place mainly to establish lines for crowd control, but I figured it was not my role to 'micro-manage' the media, even if I could. The delegation moved on to polling place 38/39, only two kilometres further to the west.

We arrived there about 12.30 pm and were advised that more than 1600 of the 1729 registered voters had voted by noon. We watched the local *bupati*, who we had not previously met, walk across to vote with a couple of tough-looking escorts. They were, no doubt, bodyguards, or maybe even 'go betweens' for the local militia. The *bupati* spoke with nobody and was through the process in less than five minutes. As the delegation moved off to return to the vehicles, I noticed some armed police nearby. The '60 Minutes' team had caught up with us for another informal interview. Beyond the TV camera I could see that we were being watched by the militia. After a while we moved on, leaving Richard Carleton and his crew talking with some locals.

At the local UNAMET headquarters, the delegation settled down for a spot of lunch (dried biscuits and cheese) by the large tree under which we had been given a briefing three days earlier. Suddenly our Indonesian police escort, Lieutenant Arly, burst into the compound to say that we should go to the local police station as there had been a major incident between Richard Carleton and a member of the militia. The Lieutenant looked particularly distressed, his smile having been replaced by a worried frown as there were now major security concerns. As we drove to the police station, I noticed the red taxi that '60 Minutes' had hired being driven in the opposite direction by a militia driver.

We arrived at Liquica Police Station to find Richard Carleton in the foyer being confronted by a local militia leader. The Indonesian police were trying to calm things down, but stood back as the militia leader went into full flight. In fact, the police were very deferential towards him as he moved from screaming point to silent scowling. Richard Carleton looked very tense.

The Second Secretary of the Australian Embassy in Jakarta, Norè Hoogstad, stepped forward with me into the foyer and used her considerable translation skills and abilities as a diplomat to try to calm the situation. Richard Carleton, who was looking a little pale (although he still had his odd smirk), said that he 'meant no harm'. Eventually, Nore managed to get an informal agreement with the police that the Australian Observer Delegation would take the '60 Minutes' team back to Dili (as they had lost the services of their taxi) so they could be dealt with directly by the Dili police. I agreed that this seemed the best way forward as surely the situation could be more easily sorted out in Dili.

As I invited Richard Carleton to ride in the back of my vehicle, and the producer, Mark Llewellyn, and two cameramen to be passengers in other vehicles, my thoughts were of the five Australian journalists killed at Balibo. I did not feel in any personal danger, but the '60 Minutes' team were.

I did not like the look of the local militia who drove past as the convoy was about to move off. I also noticed that several trucks, loaded with Indonesian armed personnel, had joined us to provide additional security. En route to Dili we came across the red taxi on the side of the road surrounded by a group of East Timorese, but for security reasons it was decided that we should drive on and not stop at any stage.

Richard Carleton and I had a terse conversation as I tried to point out to him that Liquica was a very real hotspot, where over fifty people had been massacred by militia in the church courtyard just five months previous. When Richard asked me whether I was in fact delivering him into Indonesian custody at Dili Police Station, I reminded him very sharply that we had secured an agreement to get him out of Liquica and back to Dili and that he would have to report to the Dili Police Station. I was not going to add to the difficulties of the situation, especially as UNAMET and the townspeople of Liquica had been left behind to face a militia that had suddenly become very angry, stirred up as they were by Richard Carleton's activities. It later emerged that Richard had asked several questions too many.

There was a lot of tension in the air, especially as we had been forced to cancel plans to visit a nearby polling station at Hatukesie. I did not have a great deal more to say on the journey back. We were being driven by an East Timorese and my experiences as Minister for Trade always led me to be careful in saying anything in front of local drivers. I had hoped that we could go to the Consulate first to get some further advice, but we were under escort and the Dili Police Station was the first building on the way in.

So we arrived at the main Dili Police Station to be met by a great clutter of people and vehicles. As we stood around in the compound, the '60 Minutes' team began to gather their equipment. Lieutenant Arly plus a more senior officer indicated instead that they were to go up the steps into the Police headquarters building

The Australian Observer Delegation at Dili Airport. From left to right: Craig Jacobsen, Vicki Bourne, Ann Wigglesworth, Pat Walsh, Marise Payne, Tim Fischer, Laurie Brereton, Rae Perry, Kirk Conningham, Anthony Pearce, Stephanie Shwabsky, Paul Cartwright (Photo Marise Payne)

The entrance to Hotel Turismo. The Dili waterfront can be seen in the background. (Photo Marise Payne)

CNRT graffiti on a wall in Dili next to the symbol for the 50th anniversary of Indonesian independence (top left). (Photo Anthony Pearce)

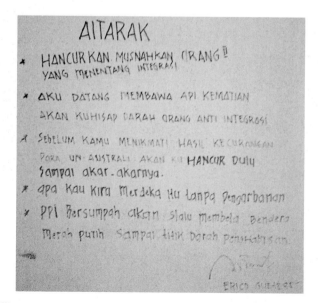

'Erico's' chilling message was found scrawled on a wall near my room at the Hotel Turismo. Despite the difference in the spelling of his name, militia leader Eurico Gueterres is believed to have written the message.

Left: Many people in Dili wore pro-autonomy t-shirts. (Photo Anthony Pearce)
Right: A pro-autonomy rally held on the day we arrived in East Timor.
(Photo Anthony Pearce)

Pro-independence supporters in Dili. The young man on the right is wearing a
Xanana Gusmao t-shirt. (Photo Anthony Pearce)

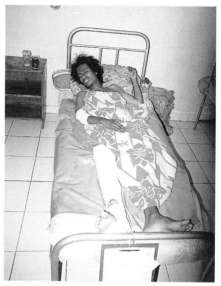

Left: Timbul Silaen, the Indonesian Police chief who was later accused by the Indonesian Human Rights Commission of ordering police to take part in the killing and destruction. (Photo Alan Mills) Right: A pro-independence supporter recovering in a private hospital from gunshot wounds received outside the CNRT headquarters in Dili on 26 August. (Photo Alan Mills)

On our arrival in East Timor we heard rumours of violence in downtown Dili. Here police attempt to control militia after they blocked the roads around the centre of Dili. (Photo Anthony Pearce)

The church in Liquica where over fifty pro-independence supporters were killed in April and where UNAMET was attacked on 4 September 1999.
(Photo Paul Mulqueeney)

Three days before the ballot, this family near Liquica were looking forward to voting. (Photo Marise Payne)

Some of UNAMET's key personnel. From left to right: Jeff Fischer,
Beng Yong Chew, Alan Mills, Ian Martin, Johannes Wortel,
Brigadier General Rezaqul Haider, David Wimhurst. (Photo Alan Mills)

With John McCarthy, the Ambassador from Central Casting, Marise Payne and
Constantino Soares, the Bupati of Gleno. (Photo Marise Payne)

With Lieutenant Paul Symon before his radio interviews. (Photo Marise Payne)

Long queues of voters waited at nearly every polling station for their chance to participate in the ballot. (Photo Alan Mills)

The UNAMET-organised press conference with leaders of the militia, Falantil and pro-independence and pro-autonomy groups a few days before the ballot. It was here that all groups declared they would ban the carrying of arms in public places on polling day. (Photo Alan Mills)

Laurie Brereton and Anthony Pearce check out a large crater in the road that could have made passing traffic an easy target for the militia. (Photo Marise Payne)

UNAMET

Do you ACCEPT the proposed special autonomy for East Timor within the Unitary State of the Republic of Indonesia?

Apakah anda MENERIMA usul otonomi khusus untuk Timor Timur di dalam Negara Kesatuan Republik Indonesia?

Ita Boot SIMU proposta autonomia espesiál ba Timor Lorosae iha Estadu Unitáriu Repúblika Indonezia nia laran?

Aceita a autonomia especial proposta para Timor Leste integrada no Estado Unitário da República da Indonésia?

ACCEPT
MENERIMA
HA'U SIMU
ACEITO

OR   ATAU   KA   OU

Do you REJECT the proposed special autonomy for East Timor, leading to East Timor's separation from Indonesia?

Apakah anda MENOLAK usul otonomi khusus Timor Timur, yang akan mengakibatkan berpisahnya Timor Timur dari Indonesia?

Ita Boot LA SIMU proposta autonomia espesiál ba Timor Lorosae, nebé sei lori Timor Lorosae atu haketak an hosi Indonezia?

Rejeita a autonomia especial proposta para Timor Leste, levando á separação de Timor Leste da Indonésia?

REJECT
MENOLAK
HA'U LA SIMU
REJEITO

The ballot paper. The top panel put the question for autonomy and the bottom panel put the question for independence. (Courtesy Australian Electoral Commission)

Vicki Bourne and I check the ballot boxes at polling place number 21. (Photo Marise Payne)

Left: Polling day at Manatuto. Voters hold up their voter registration papers and official identification. (Photo Anthony Pearce) Right: A voter in Manatuto casts her ballot. (Photo Anthony Pearce)

Lunch at Liquica just before being informed by Lieutenant Arly of the incident between Richard Carleton and the militia. (Photo Marise Payne)

Polling day and a mother and daughter hopeful for the future. (Photo Anthony Pearce)

Militia outside UNAMET's headquarters in Atsabe. It was here that eight local electoral officers were held hostage and one of their co-workers died as a result of a militia attack. (Photo Alan Mills)

Left: Geoff Hazel was wounded in trying to break the siege at Gleno. (Photo Alan Mills) Right: Alan Mills and Phil Hunter at the helicopter landing site at Atsabe. Among the locals who surrounded the site were militia with hidden weapons. (Photo Alan Mills)

The *Australian*'s Don Greenless with the 'Grumpy' cap I gave him. The cap summed up his response to Richard Carleton's conduct the previous day. (Photo Marise Payne)

Checking the unopened ballot boxes and mailbags at the counting compound the day after the ballot. (Photo Anthony Pearce)

A UNAMET team reconciling the ballot papers before the count began. (Photo Anthony Pearce)

With the ever-smiling Lieutenant Arly at the foot of the statue of Jesus Christ. (Photo Marise Payne)

Earl Candler (left) with Paul Mulqueeney (right). Militia shot Earl in the stomach as UNAMET was leaving Liquica. (Photo Paul Mulqueeney)

A UNAMET vehicle abandoned at Liquica following the attack on 4 September. (Photo Keith Randall)

Refugees in the UN's Dili compound the day after the ballot result was announced. (Photo Paul Mulqueeney)

and that the Observer Delegation should depart the compound to resume its activities.

Lieutenant Arly had done much to help get the '60 Minutes' team out of its predicament. I later found out that at one stage he jumped into the red taxi, which had been hijacked by a militia driver, to ensure that the '60 Minutes' team were taken to the local police station and not out into the jungle or down to the beach. This quick response by Lieutenant Arly helped bring some control to the situation by at least getting the '60 Minutes' crew safely to the Liquica Police Station compound. I have no doubt that if the Lieutenant had not taken this action, there was a real chance that Richard Carleton and the '60 Minutes' team may have been gravely injured or may never have been seen alive again.

I knew that we had better get moving, but I was very concerned that the '60 Minutes' team now faced some form of interrogation. Nore Hoogstad offered to accompany them into police headquarters and help out as an interpreter. It was to be at least eight hours before she was to re-emerge.

In the melee I became aware of the '60 Minutes' tapes and had to decide what to do with them. Four options ran through my mind. The first was to use Australia's diplomatic bags to get the tapes out; the second was to use the RAAF aircraft that would be carrying the delegation back to Australia. I rejected both of these ideas. The third option was to let the tapes accompany the crew in to the Dili Police Station, where they would no doubt be used as part of the interviews, or I could get the material to the Hotel Dili where '60 Minutes' was staying. I decided to take this latter option. This split-second decision may not have been correct in normal circumstances, but I thought it was better to get the tapes away from the police compound for the sake of my fellow Australians. I also considered the interests of the East Timorese voters interviewed on the tapes. I make no apology for having made that decision. I did not touch the tapes at any stage, but resolved to take full responsibility for my action.

My last view of Richard Carleton in East Timor was him leading his crew up the steps of the police station, with two cameramen looking very uncomfortable and producer Mark Llewellyn speaking urgently into a mobile phone. We went back to the Consulate to report on the incident and dictate a short summary of the events, which I knew would have many ramifications.

The '60 Minutes' team was interviewed for eight hours, with the Consul, James Batley, joining Nore Hoogstad to provide assistance and to find a way forward. Eventually the Indonesian authorities decided to deport the '60 Minutes' team, who were travelling without proper visas. The Consul had to provide a letter of recognisance vouching that Richard Carleton and his crew would go to the airport the next morning and depart the country. In what was a very busy day, Australian Consulate staff were tied up hosing down a very damaging incident that should never have occurred.

In the aftermath of the '60 Minutes' debacle, the militia formed several roadblocks and became quite aggressive in and around Liquica. The Australian delegation returning from Maliana passed through the roadblocks to have their vehicles pounded by fist-thumping militia. The job faced by the unarmed UNAMET staff in Liquica was also made a whole lot more difficult.

In reviewing the '60 Minutes' saga, I decided not to make too much of it, but there was no doubt that Richard Carleton and his crew had put other people's lives in jeopardy. They had acted irresponsibly and recklessly, as I later said in Parliament. (This was confirmed by the story aired on '60 Minutes', one week later, should any additional proof be needed. It showed Richard Carleton persisting with an interview that was obviously upsetting the militia.) However, I did resolve to write formally to the Managing Director and Chief Executive Officer of Channel 9, David Leckie, upon my return to lodge a complaint.

We wanted to get back to the business of observing, so travelled to several more polling places in Dili returning at the end of the day to polling place 21, the first polling station we had visited more that ten hours previously. There were no queues as no one was left to vote; almost all those who had registered had voted, as was the case at most other polling places. (The Maliano group, which included Laurie Brereton, reported much the same when they returned safely to Dili.) The closure of the ballot was scheduled for 4 pm and the staff looked very weary. We went through the procedure of sealing the ballot boxes, signing and witnessing the relevant forms, and observing the collection of the electoral material and marked rolls showing those who had voted. It was a smooth operation, notwithstanding a little tension between some of the polling place staff after a very long hot day.

I did some more television interviews from the rooftop of the Hotel Mahkota where a beautiful cool sea breeze was blowing. Ian Martin was also on the roof at that time and bumped me off the SBS live cross to Australia. SBS quite correctly chose to give him priority, having taken considerable footage of the Australian delegation at polling place 21 at the start of the day. I was relaxed about this and, in any event, had plenty of media to do before rejoining the group at our hotel, where we met up with some of the other delegations to swap notes.

I learnt during dinner with the New Zealand delegation at a small Portuguese restaurant that the '60 Minutes' team were still under interrogation and that Nore Hoogstad was still with them. I felt very sorry for both the Consul and the Second Secretary as they carried this extra burden on a very busy day. Indeed, it had been a very long day for all of us, but especially for those members of the delegation who had travelled all the way to Maliana and Balibo. I made a point of acknowledging them and thanking our security personnel. At the restaurant, I also had a quiet word to Australian Ambassador John McCarthy about various aspects of the day and offered him a detailed explanation about what had happened at Liquica.

We returned to the Hotel Turismo for a drink in the courtyard where Pat Walsh and Vicki Bourne tried to phone Xanana Gusmao, the independence leader who had been in jail in Jakarta for many years. Around midnight they spoke directly to him. It was a very emotional moment and Vicki burst into tears for the final time that day. Given the tension, the long hours and the excitement of the day, I thought she had done very well in maintaining her composure, as had we all.

I stepped aside from the others to write some notes on what had been an incredible day, a day that acted as a sharp reminder of how often we take democracy for granted in Australia and elsewhere.

Looking at the polling day as a whole, it was clear there had been a huge turn out. The militia had not succeeded in preventing people from voting in large numbers. The polling places had been well organised and well equipped. Against the odds, all the electoral material seemed to be on hand. The ballot paper was clear enough, with its two choices presented straight-forwardly and there seemed to be no doubt that people knew how to mark the ballot paper, either by placing a hole in the ballot paper in the square of choice or by any other form of marking. The international polling staff were very much across their responsibilities. Some local staff were overawed, especially at the beginning of the polling day, but soon overcame their nervousness. There were one or two very minor irregularities but these were quickly rectified. (For instance, some uncertainty about the correct way to cross off the voter when he or she had been identified on the master copy of the roll.) None of these irregularities could take away from the extraordinary overall efficiency, effectiveness and integrity of this very popular consultation.

As I thought about the day, I knew I could draft a statement without qualms to put before the delegation members the next morning announcing that the Australian Observer Delegation had found the vote to be, by and large, secret, free and fair. Well done to the people of East Timor!

There were some sharp differences between the vote in East Timor and voting in Australia. The people of East Timor had been through a rare and strange process with the independence ballot having real life and death ramifications. Never in Australia has there been a referendum or an election to compare in magnitude or uniqueness with the East Timor ballot. To some extent this explained why my experience in East Timor felt so incredibly different to election day in Australia. I contested seven Lower House elections for the New South Wales Parliament (representing part of the Riverina between 1971 and 1984) before moving on to the Federal arena at age 38 to successfully fight six elections for the seat of Farrer. Despite all of this campaigning, including the very emotional times associated with the Dismissal and double dissolution of the Federal parliament in 1975, nothing prepared me for what I witnessed on Monday 30 August in East Timor. The differences were myriad, but overarching all was the look of exhilaration (which was sometimes touched with fear) on the faces of many of the voters. I thought how lucky and privileged I had been to witness 'democracy at work' in these extraordinary and difficult circumstances. The people of East Timor were deciding their future through the ballot box.

By the time Monday night came around, there was, of course, one other minor difference and that was the absence of a tally-room with all of its emotion, drama, bright lights and tension. It is in a tally-room during a very close election that the full thrill of democracy in action is experienced. Here in East Timor there was to be no counting at the polling places and all of the ballot boxes were to be sent back to the counting centre in Dili. Over the next day and late into the week, after verification and double-checking of the roll, the real count would begin.

I thought somewhat sadly that the advent of the Internet and the immediate posting of progressive counts might soon eclipse the tally-room in Australia. I resolved if there was no longer going to be a tally-room, then there would be no Tim Fischer contesting elections. Mind you, with thirteen successful elections under my belt, the fourteenth might just be testing my luck too much.

For the people in East Timor, it did not matter if there was a tally-room or not. Over 400 000 votes had been cast and, with tension building, they just wanted to know the official result.

Back in my room, and absolutely exhausted, I found

a Violet Crumble Bar and demolished it. I dived into the cold shower, crawled into bed and crashed into a deep sleep, but not before realising that I had forgotten to take my daily malaria tablet. Having had malaria thirty years ago, I was not going to take any risks even with all the polling day excitement. So I reached out for the bitter tablet and swallowed hard, but this minor act of awful necessity did not mar my thoughts at the end of this truly historic and extraordinary day.

SEVEN

RECOVERY DAY

Tuesday 31 August 1999

THE DAY BEGAN early with an informal meeting of the delegation to discuss all that we had witnessed on polling day and to prepare the statement for the press conference I had called for midmorning. The general feeling was that the ballot procedures in and around the polling places we visited had been conducted with efficiency and integrity. (Other international observers we contacted held similar views.) At this stage we could only speculate what the result might be, but a number of my colleagues thought the huge turnout would almost certainly favour independence. To my surprise, given the heavy-handed tactics of the militia, nobody thought the secrecy of the ballot had been compromised. In fact, one member of the delegation had been quickly directed away from the polling screen when an official thought he was too close. No one was permitted to observe how people were marking their ballot papers.

Marise Payne pointed out that because some people

had folded their ballot papers once rather than twice, it may have been possible to see how they voted as they placed their voting paper in the ballot box. However, as this would have been in breach of all UNAMET regulations for observer delegations, she was not tempted to undertake any informal 'scrutineering', something that is practised by all political parties on election day in Australia. Councillor Rae Perry remarked that she thought the processes around the polling places had been incredibly good, given the difficult and congested conditions.

It was decided to adopt the formal statement I had drafted the previous evening. I was very happy that the delegation was unanimous about this, but Pat Walsh and some of the others were concerned that the '60 Minutes' saga should not get in the way of Australian reporting of the extraordinary and happy scenes of thousands of East Timorese voting. I agreed with his sentiments and said that I would make a special effort to see that the story was kept in perspective by the rest of the media. The only practical way I could do this was by being careful with the language I used.

I suspected that Richard Carleton would put maximum spin on the events to suggest that he had been somehow wronged, thereby besmirching me in the process. Bitter experience had taught me to keep a record of events and meetings that had the potential to become controversial, and I had done so on this occasion.

The media returned from their morning briefing and press conference with the UNAMET staff to report that voter turnout had been very high right across East Timor. We found a shady corner of the Hotel Turismo courtyard to hold out 'doorstop' press conference and I invited the delegation to stand with me as I made a short opening statement.

I formally announced that the Australian Observer Delegation was satisfied with the process to this stage, that the ballot had been secret, free and fair and that it had been conducted with incredible efficiency and integrity, given the very difficult conditions. I congratulated UNAMET, including the military liaison officers and CIVPOL, in helping to bring this about. I congratulated the poll workers who had come from around the world, and particularly commended the locally engaged staff.

However, I warned that there were uncertain times ahead particularly after the announcement of the results of the ballot in a few days time. I then handed over to my colleagues. Laurie Brereton spoke of his concerns regarding the security situation over the next few weeks. This was backed up by other delegation members who called for armed peace-keepers to be brought in as soon as possible.

Marise Payne pointed out that there was a high turnout at polling places in the critical border area adjoining Indonesian West Timor. The delegation not only visited a number of peaceful polling places in the area, but also the house in Balibo where the Australian journalists were killed.

As the press conference ended, several of the longer-term journalists in Dili expressed their anger over Richard Carleton's conduct the previous day. The extra tension around Liquica after the Carleton incident had heightened their concern for Australian journalists.

Lindsay Murdoch from the Fairfax press, said that he would be writing a piece on the luxurious trappings Richard Carleton travelled with, including his smoked salmon, champagne and esky. Another journalist angrily exclaimed that 'this guy flies in, pushes hard, gets a "gee whiz" story, and then immediately flies out—leaving others to work through the mess left behind'. I did nothing to discourage their robust thoughts on the matter. When I gave *Australian* journalist Don Greenlees a spare cap with the word 'Grumpy' embroidered across its front to shield his very sunburnt head, he confessed he was feeling very grumpy that morning, particularly about his journalistic colleague Richard Carleton.

It was while thinking about how East Timor would be reported that the idea of writing a book giving my impressions of the ballot process came to mind. Aware that I was operating without personal staff for the first time in many years whilst on a working visit overseas, I had kept reasonably comprehensive notes and collected a good deal of material. I decided I would make up my mind as soon as I got home so that the memories were fresh and reasonably accurate.

The press conference ended and the delegation travelled downtown to the Consulate. Along the way we saw some of the remnants of roadblocks that had been erected the previous day by the militia. This reminder of the militia's presence was very timely for our meeting with the Ambassador, and the military liaison and consular staff to discuss the security situation and all that we had seen over the last few days.

Reports were coming in that in the aftermath of the poll, the militia were becoming active once more, and were attempting to block the return of the ballot boxes. I thought this indicated that they believed the huge turnout of voters meant a strong vote for independence. There was a report from Gleno, where we had been the previous Saturday, that a siege was taking place in the hills nearby to prevent some of the ballot boxes being transferred back to Dili.

The Australian Consulate was impressive by Dili standards. It had been an Indonesian Insurance office until the Australian Government had recently negotiated its use as the consular office. Handily located on the main street in from the airport, the original high fence was being reinforced by Australian contractors who were adding several rolls of barbed wire. Access to and from the building was through a well-guarded gate. No chances were being taken with security.

The Australian staff were working very long hours, day and night, monitoring developments and facilitating the activities of the Australian Observer Delegation. They bedded down in rooms large and small scattered through the building and were using the one bathroom and kitchen. Surveying the conditions, Vicki Bourne remarked how unfair the popular image of embassy and consular life was. Certainly those on posting to Dili were a very long way from the cocktail parties and the long lunches, the kind of lurks that in fact no longer exist on the serious diplomatic circuit.

After years of scrutinising various Ambassadors closely to assess their performance and to ensure that I was not being snowed, I had developed enormous respect for our Foreign Affairs and Trade personnel, particularly during my time as Minister for Trade. Time and time again I saw first-hand their dedication beyond the call of duty. There were some exceptions, but these were very few—one or two square-peg ambassadors in round-hole postings (one even traded luxury cars illegally), but the system soon sorted them out. DFAT had also demonstrated an ability to move on from past policy practices, at least in the trade arena where, during my period as Minister, they boosted bilateral trade efforts whilst continuing to pursue the regional and the multilateral. Here in Dili, the diplomatic team worked under great pressure and, at times, their own lives were put at risk.

During our visit to the consulate we again discussed the deteriorating security situation. There was no doubt that the militia were becoming bolder, but within parameters—the airport runway was clearly off limits to militia attack. I began to worry more about what lay ahead for East Timor.

We took the opportunity of a working lunch to lay down the format and content of the formal report we would be making to Alexander Downer upon our return. There was no dispute and, given the diversity of views long held by members of the delegation over East Timor, this was an achievement.

As the delegation prepared to move off to visit Caritas headquarters, I chose to have my left ear attended to at the consular clinic. Politicians are always accused of not listening carefully; my problem was that a narrowing channel to the eardrum made it increasingly difficult for me to hear. The irritation level was at times intense, but this was not one of the main reasons why I decided to step down from the front bench and my post as Deputy Prime Minister, as some have speculated. In fact there were several factors including family and the hell of constant travel. I received efficient attention and had what seemed like 44 gallons of water syringed through my ear. I could hear a lot better and felt equipped for the rest of our visit.

During the treatment, I recalled an army general in Vietnam who was totally deaf in his right ear. The less than bold junior officers reporting on operations at the daily briefing all sat to the general's right as he rarely asked questions of those on his deaf side. However, one day the general woke up to this ploy and forced those officers to move directly in front of him. Whilst seating arrangements and the like are minor aspects of group management and leadership, I confess I used all the standard tricks, such as sitting up front, to build the degree of control required as delegation leader.

It was quite hot as we drove to the Caritas head-quarters, located near the main Dili Cathedral, for an early afternoon meeting that had been arranged by Ann Wigglesworth. Caritas was housed in a modest single-storey building with a long central passage and a functional layout. We met with several volunteers and with Father Francisco Barreto, the organisation's head who would be reported 'missing feared killed' for many weeks after the ballot result was announced. We were briefed on the numerous education and health problems Caritas was confronting and were shown a storage room, with its limited range of pharmaceuticals, and some of the other modest facilities. Clearly, despite huge efforts, Caritas and many other organisations simply could not cope with the demand on their scarce resources. I was forcibly reminded of the great value of even small amounts of aid, especially in fighting diseases such as malaria and TB. Caritas appeared lean and efficient, unlike the luxury four-wheel drive world outfits where charity begins at headquarters and rarely gets out to the field.

While the main task of the delegation was over, another task was about to begin. We wanted to observe the return of the ballot boxes and the count. The need for continuing independent observation of this part of the process would be critical in gaining international acceptance for the ballot outcome. As only one observer per delegation was permitted entry, we split up and I went off with Anthony Pearce to the compound where all the ballot boxes had been deposited, under guard, and where the vote counting would take place.

A small group of delegation members went to tour downtown Dili and do some shopping in preparation for the return home late the following day. While they were visiting the market, a militia group formed and began advancing along the street with machetes and guns barely concealed underneath their shirts. The ever-efficient Lieutenant Arly quickly moved the group back to their vehicles and out of the area. The situation continued to be volatile (indeed the group had been forced to take a very circuitous route to avoid new roadblocks), but thanks to our security detail no one was harmed. We were given security support in many ways, not all of which we saw first-hand. There was much negotiation and surveillance away from our view.

I arrived at the counting compound, an octagonal museum building that had obviously been built by Jakarta as a gesture to placate the East Timorese. It must have been the ultimate insult for some in Jakarta that this museum was now being used for the counting of the ballot that would determine East Timor's future. I was very concerned that the surrounding fence was only about two and a half metres high as it could have been breached without too much difficulty. If an attempt were made to torch the counting centre over the next few days, the efforts of thousands upon thousands would be destroyed.

UNAMET had arranged for two teams of about 30 each to process the ballot papers over two long shifts. These were international staff and their work was to be monitored by the chief electoral officers from Ireland, South Africa and Korea and by one representative of each observer delegation.

I bumped into the Chief Electoral Officer, Jeff Fischer, in the forecourt and he told me that all the ballot boxes and mailbags, with related material such as the marked-off electoral rolls, had been returned from the polling places. I was shown a mailbag with blood-stains that had come from Atsabe where two local staffers had been killed. I resolved to make more enqui-ries about this incident.

Jeff Fischer looked absolutely exhausted and had

every right to be. I left him in peace and moved on to talk to some of the supervisors and to inspect first-hand the seals on the 850 ballot boxes. I looked for the ballot boxes from polling place number 21, the first polling place we attended on polling day. The seals were all intact and there was no damage to the boxes. However, this was not the case with one of the ballot boxes from the Gleno area, which had been damaged by helicopter down draught.

I could not believe how quickly key material had been returned to Dili. All of the ballot boxes had been recovered from islands, remote villages and towns large and small by late afternoon Tuesday. There was no way this could have been stage-managed for the benefit of observers, as the polling places and supporting documentation were all cross-referenced. Moreover, over a thousand independent observers had been at almost all of the polling places to witness the operation first-hand.

As we watched the detailed checking off of the ballot boxes before the count proper commenced, I asked for permission to take some photos of what was 'pure democratic gold', material evidence of choice expressed through the ballot. For a moment I felt very emotional, in wonderment of all that had been achieved against the odds. I noticed that Jeff Fischer had collapsed on a bench in the corner and was fast asleep. I think he had been on the go for 36 hours, so I did not disturb him. I took my leave with Anthony Pearce and travelled back to join the others.

The delegation was keen to host a dinner to thank the Ambassador and the Consul and their teams, the military liaison officers, the Indonesian Police escort and our own Federal Police agents. We also wanted to invite Jim Dunn who had been an Australian Consul to Dili in the seventies. The only place to eat was the open, tin shed fish restaurant we had been to previously, but would it be safe to leave the hotel compound on the first night after polling day? Opinion was divided, although eventually, after the Indonesian Police had negotiated a local 'peace pact' with a group of militia located in a house near the restaurant, it was decided that the dinner could go ahead. These negotiations again demonstrated how cosy the relationship was between the militia and the police.

There was an enjoyable mix of delegation members and guests sitting at the long trestle table, with the Federal Police and Indonesian security personnel at an adjoining table. Once again, the fish and rice were very tasty and we were fortified by some good Australian wine that DFAT had somehow managed to get through to East Timor. (This was a most welcome, but tiny component of the $1 billion worth of wine that Australia now exports annually.) I commended them on this logistical achievement and recalled the time some Australian wine, packed in a container of books, failed to make it to our Embassy in Iran a number of years ago. Apparently the religious police, noticing that the books had sprung a leak, followed the container to its delivery point at the Embassy, and carried out an inspection. You can imagine the staff frustration as the entire liquid content of the container was whisked away just a couple of metres short of the diplomatic compound. The sodden books were allowed through though. It was a very dry Christmas for those Australian diplomats in Iran who had been without certain supplies for many months. Luckily this was not the case for our final dinner in East Timor.

The dinner was a great success and we all started to relax a little. I invited everybody to some say words, but particularly Jim Dunn. This brave old man was staying with an East Timorese family some distance from the protection afforded by the well-presented Australian

Consulate and the key hotels. He did not think he was in any danger, but he was deeply concerned for the East Timorese family whom he had known from his previous posting many years ago. He subsequently wrote that one of the hardest things he'd ever had to do was say goodbye to this family as they pleaded with him to take their children to Darwin.

Jim Dunn reminded us that there had been fighting in East Timor for many years, even before the Indonesian invasion. That the vote took place among scenes of amazing harmony and happiness, held out some hope for an end to the violence. But what of East Timor's future? Most around the table believed that the immediate period after the announcement of the result would be most critical for what would either be a fledgling nation, or an autonomous province of Indonesia.

Brigadier Jim Molan, Colonel Ken Brownrigg from the Embassy Defence Attaché Unit and Colonel Paul Symon told the dinner that there had been, by and large, very good relations between the people of many different nationalities working in UNAMET and CIVPOL. I wished this had been the case with some of our media, when I realised that Nore Hoogstad was missing from the dinner. She was still recovering from the eight hours she had spent the previous day with the Indonesian Police negotiating a way out for the '60 Minutes' team.

I thanked everybody for the enormous support they had provided to the delegation and said that we would be giving the popular consultation a clean bill of health when reporting to Alexander Downer. The parliamentarians in the delegation decided to shout dinner and settled the bill by way of a series of currency swaps. Back in my room at the Hotel Turismo, I had a swag of requests for interviews, including one from the 'Today Show' for a phone link live-to-air (at 5 am the following morning!). I readily agreed to this, especially as it came from Channel 9, the same network on which '60 Minutes' is broadcast.

As I turned in for one last time in Dili, I thought optimistically that perhaps not only would the counting proceed as smoothly as the vote had, but that the results would also be accepted. Unfortunately, the more pessimistic side of me said that there was a good deal of evidence around to suggest otherwise. I was to be both right and wrong. The militia were not going to roll over quietly, and already Indonesia was taking steps to top up militia weapons and ammunition stocks.

EIGHT

DEPARTURE FROM DILI

Wednesday 1 September 1999

A T 4.50 AM my mobile phone rang and I woke with
a jolt as Channel 9's 'Today Show' team checked
out the line and asked whether I was ready to do the
live cross with Steve Liebmann in 15 minutes time. I
said I was awake (half-awake at any rate) and awake
enough to ask, on this occasion, for one condition —a
question from Steve on the '60 Minutes' saga. Steve, as
the professional and clear-sighted anchorman he is, said
he would be happy to ask the question, but pointed
out there had been a lot of coverage already, including
Richard Carleton's claim that he had done no wrong.

To conserve the phone's battery I hung up, using
the few minutes before the interview to work out some
key points—always a wise approach when doing an
interview from outside Australia in the middle of the
night or in the early early morning. In fact, my general
rule had always been never to do TV programs such as
'Sunday' from overseas without being thoroughly

briefed first. Too often they were disasters waiting to happen, as I could never be sufficiently up-to-date on every nuance of every breaking story. I remember Bob McMullan, the then Minister for Trade, once doing the Laurie Oakes 'Sunday' segment from the Philippines. Bob is normally a competent performer in the 'thoughtful interview setting', but on this occasion the interview was a complete disaster both in presentation and content. The lighting was all wrong, there was a slight sound delay due to a poor satellite connection, and the interview was prerecorded 12 hours before going to air so was stale on the issues of the day.

Needless to say, I was able to respond crisply to Steve's questions and to affirm that the ballot had been, in the view of the delegation, secret, free and fair. I filled out my answers with some local colour and information on the collection of the ballot boxes, adding that the counting was about to commence in earnest after reconciliation of the polling place returns.

True to his word, Steve asked about the '60 Minutes' incident and I said that Richard Carleton's actions had caused deep concern and he had been deported. Whilst I had not felt in any personal danger, the incident was very unfortunate and had been the result of Richard Carleton's conduct. The interview ended on this note, and I felt a whole lot better for having made this point as firmly as I could. I knew that Richard Carleton would be putting maximum spin on his story now that he was safely back in Sydney.

I also learnt from other media calls that morning that some of the print journalists in Dili, particularly those from the Fairfax press, had examined Richard Carleton's baggage at the Hotel Dili. This led to newspaper headlines such as 'CAVIAR WARRIOR' and 'CHAMPAGNE JOURNALISM', as Richard's practice of carrying an esky full of the best cheeses and pâtés and so forth was laid bare. I smiled, but knew there would be another bitter round or two on this matter. I also remembered the admonition of Pat Walsh and others that we should work to ensure the '60 Minutes' saga did not become the story. I thought on balance this was unlikely to happen, as the significance of this historic vote now had long overdue world media attention. The sheer scale of the event would ensure that the Australian media stayed with the main game.

I quickly packed my bags. As always, I had brought too much luggage, but I had been uncertain about what to expect on the ground in Dili. I had included a couple of books, Sir Edmund Hillary's excellent *View from the Summit*, and a book on Bhutan, but found no time to even glance at them in the hurly-burly of delegation activity. I settled my account, which had been carefully and accurately kept in a handwritten ledger maintained by the hard-working hotel staff, and I wished them the very best.

As only one delegate per observer delegation was allowed into the counting compound at any one time (and I had already had the privilege), our delegation had time to see something of Dili on this last morning. We decided to travel out to the base of the Jesus Christ statue, then to a World War II memorial, and on to see the Santa Cruz Cemetery where the Dili massacre had taken place.

As luck would have it, we met up with our New Zealand friends in the carpark at the famous statue at the base of the headland. This delegation was also winding up its activities and preparing to travel on to Jakarta and then back to New Zealand. Despite including a representative from just about every party that had a seat in the New Zealand Parliament (and there were many), the New Zealanders had also settled down to become a cohesive and hard-working delegation.

I walked up the grand pathway to the statue and found that the Stations of the Cross had been carefully laid out, with each Station placed about 50 metres or so along the path in small grottos. As a less-than-perfect practising Catholic, I studied each of the Stations with interest for a few seconds and said a silent prayer. I was hesitant in doing this as we had been told repeatedly that the East Timorese bitterly resented this project because it had been forced on them by President Soeharto. For my part, I found the scene extraordinarily tranquil, and the Stations of the Cross simple and not too 'over the top'. It was also a chance to do a bit of physically demanding walking at long last.

At the end of the path we came to a large artificially created plateau with a small altar at the northern end. Someone remarked that this is probably where President Soeharto landed in his helicopter, as he would not have dared risk driving through Dili when he came for the dedication of the statue. We pushed on, up a flight of steps to the base of this incredible statue, which stands about 27 metres high—apparently a subtle point to emphasise that East Timor was the 27th province of Indonesia. As I stood on the platform at the base of this towering statue and looked along the coastline past Dili, I wondered whether it was now just a matter of weeks before East Timor ceased to be an Indonesian province.

Then a magic moment occurred. I noticed that the globe representing the planet Earth was missing New Zealand in its entirety, and Tasmania for that matter too. I took much joy in pointing this out to the Kiwis, who argued strenuously that as New Zealand would have been where the support pillar joined the structure, there had been no deliberate oversight. They had a point, because the support pillar joined the globe just east of Australia and the globe provided the base for Jesus Christ's feet which, in turn, obliterated parts of

South America. Unfortunately there was plenty of space for Tasmania, so once again our Apple Isle had been completely overlooked.

All our East Timorese friends showed a great distaste, if not contempt, for the whole complex, notwithstanding that most of them were Catholics and, in other circumstances, would have been enormously respectful of the Stations of the Cross and the statue of Jesus Christ. Somewhat facetiously, I thought one possible reason the East Timorese might have to demolish this statue rather than rededicate it could be to rectify the mistake in not showing Tasmania.

After some photographs, we moved on to the memorial plaque that honoured the links between Australians, the Portuguese and the East Timorese in World War II. The plaque sits in a picturesque setting next to a school about 1000 metres above sea level and overlooks Dili and the airport zone to the west, and the road to Manatuto to the east.

On the way down, we drove past the official Governor's residence, built to have commanding views over most of Dili. For some reason, the Indonesians had made little use of this quite grand residence, which was to be trashed in the aftermath of the announcement of the ballot result. On the road from the memorial to the Santa Cruz Cemetery we saw many possible ambush sites, a reminder of just how volatile the situation was despite out pleasant morning of sight-seeing.

As cemeteries go, the Santa Cruz Cemetery was tidy and reasonably well maintained. But even though the morning was warm and the garden setting was pleasant, there was a chill about the place with its sad history. There are conflicting reports as to the exact number of people massacred there some eight years ago. Gareth Evans, who was Minister for Foreign Affairs at the time, played down the numbers, but it is generally accepted that well over 100 East Timorese were killed and some were pursued into the hospital and dealt with there. I was pleased to leave this sad place.

I checked security on the route back with the military liaison officers, who informed me that there had been some difficulties near the airport because of a big militia funeral procession that morning. As Marise Payne had arranged for CIVPOL to come by the hotel to provide an account of both what became known as the Gleno siege and the murder at nearby Atsabe, security was very much on our minds.

I listened very carefully as two members of the CIVPOL team recounted the events of the previous day. The militia had surrounded the Gleno UNAMET headquarters. Throughout the night they stoned the building where the ballot boxes had been stored after the close of polling the previous afternoon. A number of local staff who had camped in front of the headquarters building had been forced to move inside, and CIVPOL stood guard maintaining a picket right through the night.

The events near Atsabe had been particularly chilling, as it was here that the first locally engaged UNAMET officer had been murdered by the militia. The horrible events began at the conclusion of polling the afternoon before when UNAMET and CIVPOL officials, together with a number of locals, had been attacked by the militia. CIVPOL managed to rescue nearly everyone, but a local schoolteacher was badly wounded, and a locally employed UNAMET electoral officer was killed. Sadly, one of those rescued had also been wounded and died overnight from blood loss at the tiny UNAMET headquarters at Atsabe.

Alan Mills' task on arrival at Atsabe was to: negotiate access to the crime scene so an investigation could be carried out; negotiate the lifting of the siege; negotiate the release of the eight locals, who were next in line to be killed; and secure removal of the ballot boxes that had been left behind in the turmoil of the previous day. There was a great deal of tension in the air. Alan Mills used all his skills of patience and bluff while the Indonesian Police looked daggers at him, determined to be as uncooperative as possible. When Australian CIVPOL officers, Station Sergeant Philip Hunter and Sergeant Max Knoth (who had courageously held the post during the siege), indicated that they would not leave without the local staff, Alan asked them to quietly move their local staff to the landing pad.

A second helicopter arrived and the eight locals, under very real threat of being murdered, ran at full pelt and jumped into the aircraft, which rapidly departed. This manoeuvre added to the fury of the Indonesians and the militia. Negotiations continued and eventually, through dint of very brave and very hard work, Alan Mills and his team were able to secure the ballot boxes and gain an agreement for the siege of international UN staff to be lifted. He was, however, unable to get access to the murder scene.

In the helicopter, Alan Mills, who was going on to Dili with the ballot boxes, gave the Ermera POLRI Chief a written directive to lift all roadblocks in the Ermera/Atsabe/Gleno area. He did not know at this stage that there was trouble around Gleno and that tension had increased throughout the Ermera district.

In Gleno, another UNAMET helicopter was to make an attempt at around 8.40 am to recover the ballot boxes, which had been loaded into four-wheel-drive vehicles. The landing zone had been switched to a nearby dry riverbed to avoid the militia. However, when the militia saw the helicopter divert, they immediately started to move around to the second landing zone. The aircraft landed, but there was a delay in opening the doors to receive the ballot boxes. Compounded by some last-minute confusion, critical minutes were lost during which the militia descended on the riverbed firing their guns. The helicopter pilot followed operational regulations and lifted off, without the ballot boxes.

Suddenly, Geoffrey Hazel and his CIVPOL team were left standing in front of the ballot boxes without weapons, staring down the rapidly advancing militia. Their only protection against the guns of the militia was the thin blue cloth of the CIVPOL uniform. It was a very tense stand-off: gun-toting militia, determined to wreck the ballot by capturing ballot boxes versus Geoffrey Hazel and the Gleno CIVPOL team determined to protect them. One box had blown open under the helicopter down draught, but in a superhuman effort all but two ballot papers were recovered. The militia hesitated; the unarmed and exhausted CIVPOL team stood their ground. The minutes ticked away and then the militia blinked, and backed off enough so that eventually CIVPOL was able to reload the vehicles with the ballot boxes and return to the Gleno UNAMET headquarters.

Undoubtedly, the militia thought that they had the upper hand and expected the CIVPOL team to take off into the bushes, leaving the ballot boxes behind to be destroyed. However, after some further delay, the UNAMET helicopter made another fast approach to the main landing zone, and the boxes were loaded very quickly to be taken back to Dili.

The militia, who had been moved from the main landing zone by POLRI before the boxes were lifted, then established roadblocks at all entry points to the town. They also burnt five houses to the ground as they continued on their rampage. UNAMET staff could not get out of the town.

Lengthy negotiations were conducted throughout the afternoon with pro-autonomy leaders. Geoffrey Hazel decided to track down the local *bupati*, Dr Constantino Soares, to directly negotiate clearance for a convoy of vehicles to travel from Gleno back to Dili. Eventually, at around 5.30 pm and after several false starts, the convoy moved off, negotiated its way through several roadblocks, and later that night reached the safety of Dili.

The siege was over, the locally engaged staff had been rescued from an extremely dangerous situation and the ballot boxes had been protected. All this had been achieved against considerable odds.

Many people were involved in retrieving the situation at Atsabe and in breaking the siege at Gleno. At Atsabe, unarmed CIVPOL personnel, Phil Hunter and Max Knoth, had to carry ballot boxes up 22 exposed stairs with automatic gunshot being fired over their heads. They also treated one of the wounded and carried him up the steps into a small building where he died shortly afterwards. Their outstanding bravery was matched by the Gleno CIVPOL team, including team leader Geoffrey Hazel who had been wounded in the dry creekbed but continued to carry on with his duties the entire day and beyond. Geoffrey was supported by Kiwis Wayne Corbett and Rob Mills, Americans Randy Martenet and Jim France, along with fellow Aussies Paul Morris, Don Barnby and the newly arrived Peter Watt. All deserve recognition for their outstanding and courageous service. However, the courage and determination shown at the Gleno siege and at Atsabe was replicated many times elsewhere in East Timor. I learnt that the militia had acted in a similar way on the island of Atauro, just to the north of Dili, and that UNAMET staff were just as brave in protecting local polling officers and the ballot boxes.

I also learnt much later that the previous night an Irish TV team, led by Jerry O'Callaghan, had been interrogated for several hours by a local Indonesian Army commandant who knew all about the '60 Minutes' saga involving 'Richard Carleton and Tim Fischer and the Australian Observer Delegation'. At one stage during the interrogation, the commandant claimed that it was his duty to maintain links with and to help the militia. Clearly the security situation was beginning to deteriorate and the more pessimistic predictions would be realised.

We decided to make an early departure from the Hotel Turismo choosing to travel to the airport along waterfront roads, away from downtown Dili. While the vehicles were being loaded with our gear, I asked our security officer, Craig Jacobsen, if I could walk across to the beach in front of the hotel to take one last look along the Dili foreshore. The beach was virtually empty, although earlier that morning, as on most mornings, a few civilians jogged and walked its length, seemingly oblivious to all that had been raging in Dili over the last few days. I surmised these were international workers and visitors. It was a surreal farewell scene: behind me the bustle of vehicles, and in front of me a few beachwalkers, some coastal ferries and an Indonesian patrol boat out at sea. I could hear no shooting and again became optimistic. It might just be possible, I thought, for a clear-cut result to be accepted by everyone once and for all. 'Steady on,' I said to myself as I left the beach and clear sea waters behind, 'this whole business of East Timor has a long way to go yet'.

It was with mixed emotions that I realised I was saying goodbye to Dili and to East Timor after just one week on the ground. I knew I had been privileged to be there during this momentous week when the people of East Timor voted in their thousands for a genuine choice about their future. This was also the view of my fellow delegation members.

At the airport there was a small ceremony in front of the VIP departure lounge. The Indonesian Police, who had accompanied us throughout the week, lined up with their unit commander, Lieutenant Arly. I made a point of shaking their hands, wishing them well, and praising their efforts in Liquica, in particular. These comments were echoed by other members of the delegation. We didn't exchange gifts as the delegation had thanked our Indonesian police detail by way of the dinner the night before. It was one of those awkward moments when I wondered if an additional gesture should have been made (and perhaps it was by the consulate staff). The normal token gift, a gold-coloured kangaroo badge or pin, seemed rather inadequate in the circumstances. Also, I doubted if the Indonesians would want to face their peers wearing such a pin; widespread and growing hostility to Australia and to Australians was already starting to emerge throughout Indonesia.

I jokingly reminded one of the Australian consulate staff of an awkward legacy attached to the pins. Twenty years ago a certain Federal Member of Parliament had used them to pay for the services of a lady of the night, saying they were pure gold. He gave her one pin for each of the five nights of the Caribbean conference he was attending. Imagine his horror, when at the airport on the day of departure he found 'his friend' waiting with an inspector of police. He was presented with a choice—pay $US1000 on the spot as a kind of fine or face arrest and jail for misstating the value of the cheap pin. As Barry Cohen, retired Labor Member for Robertson, tells this story, the offending member paid up and departed on time.

Anyhow, I held on to my supply of kangaroo pins and moved into the terminal for the final immigration and customs clearance. On behalf of the delegation I gave one more farewell speech of thanks and then broke off to have a quiet talk with the Ambassador, who noticed that I had overlooked mentioning immigration officer, José Alvarez, who had also assisted our passport processing. True to type and because he is a very good ambassador, John McCarthy went over and spoke to José to make up for the oversight and to commend him for his work. I also went over to shake the immigration officer's hand.

John and I continued our discussion of the situation at the end of the seven-day visit: tension was rapidly building, and the Indonesian Army and the Indonesian Police were either unable to control the situation or simply wanted to turn a blind eye. As we walked out to the tarmac, I reflected that Dili Airport seemed to be the one piece of infrastructure that had been kept functioning in everyone's interests. I was very glad of this, but wondered why it was that the Indonesians could deliver security here with absolute success, but could not maintain security at other key locations in Dili and beyond? The answer, in truth, was ugly. They could, of course, but chose another course, that of lawlessness, death and destruction.

We settled down quickly into our seats and the RAAF Falcon jet began a long taxi for its steep take-off. I breathed a sigh of relief: we were all alive and well and in the safe hands of the number 34 Squadron Leader, Wing Commander Peter Wood.

The last glimpse I had of Dili through the aircraft window was of the museum building where the ballot boxes and ballot papers were being processed prior to the formal count. The only armed security at the compound was that provided by the Indonesian Police and the Indonesian Army. I wondered, would the militia try to break in and destroy the ballot papers on which the future of East Timor depended? As there had been no direct attack on the counting compound, even at this late stage, the militia may still have believed there was a chance of getting close to 50 per cent of the vote. Or had the Indonesian Government given assurances that an unfavourable vote would be ignored?

Mind you, the militia would not be unduly troubled by the ballot outcome. They had already selected towns to be razed to the ground, despite the precautions UNAMET had taken against retaliation. (Part of the count process was to mix the ballot papers to ensure that particular towns and villages couldn't be singled out as having voted for independence.)

Just one hour later we were on descent into Darwin where the delegation had one last doorstop interview. Clearly, national media interest was cranking up—several journalists from down south who had never been to Darwin were on hand for this doorstop. I repeated the delegation's finding that the popular consultation had been secret, free and fair, but also provided more information on the '60 Minutes' saga when asked. To try to ensure that this story would not dominate the reporting, I told the gathered media about the Gleno siege. It was then a quick phone call to home to tell Judy and the boys that I was safely back in Australia, and all on board for the last leg of the journey from Darwin to Canberra.

Just as the plane was about to start taxiing, I received a phone call to say that as part of his defence, Richard Carleton had decided to reveal my alleged complicity with '60 Minutes' in getting the TV tapes out of East Timor. I immediately decided to step right up to the line and make all of the facts known very quickly indeed. I rang ABC Radio's 'PM' and ABC News as the plane continued its taxi to the southern end of the enormously long main runway at Darwin's civil and military airport. I explained in terms designed to repulse Richard Carleton's attack, that I had been faced with four options and, all things considered, had chosen to get the tapes out of the police compound and back to the Hotel Dili where the '60 Minutes' crew had been staying. I explained that I did not believe it would have been correct to use the diplomatic bag or a RAAF aircraft to bring the tapes back, nor did I believe that it would have been correct to send them to the police station while Richard Carleton and his crew were being interviewed. My decision to respond quickly and strongly to Richard Carleton's most recent attempt to twist the story proved to be correct: I got a fair run and won a good deal of support for my decision.

I sat back and tucked in to a great meal, enjoying a good deal of banter with the RAAF flight crew. Halfway through the flight Marise Payne, Laurie Brereton and Vicki Bourne, backed up by the other delegation members, presented me with a wooden carving of a steam engine they had found in a shop in downtown Dili. It was immediately judged as a worthwhile gift for the delegation leader. My keen support for the railways is well-known, as is my oft-repeated statement that a steel wheel on a steel rail has one-seventh of the friction of a rubber-tyred wheel on a bitumen surface. I was touched by this thoughtful gesture. It was a toast all round.

One week after departing Canberra, we again stepped out into the cold night air at Fairbairn Airport. We had all returned a good deal wiser and very much wearier. The seventh day had been as eventful as all the others and it brought to an end the delegation's responsibilities, other than reporting formally to Alexander Downer. Sadly, for thousands of others, the real agony of East Timor was just beginning.

NINE

THE UGLY POSTSCRIPT

THE UNAMET BALLOT paper asked two very specific questions in four languages (Tetum, Portuguese, Indonesian and English). The English version read, 'Do you ACCEPT the proposed special autonomy for East Timor within the Unitary State of the Republic of Indonesia?'. Alongside this question was a map of East Timor showing an Indonesian flag and some related Indonesian symbols. The second question asked, 'Do you REJECT the proposed special autonomy for East Timor, leading to East Timor's separation from Indonesia?'. Attached to this option was again a slightly larger map of East Timor with the CNRT flag clearly in place.

On Saturday 4 September 1999, the result of the ballot was announced simultaneously in Dili and New York by both UNAMET and the UN. Some 451 792 voters (in East Timor and across the world) had stepped forward to register for the popular consultation. Of these, 98.8 per cent turned out to vote with 344 580 (78.5 per cent) being in favour of independence and 94 388 (21.5 per cent) in favour of special autonomy within the sovereignty of Indonesia. The UN Secretary-General, Kofi Annan, said that the UN would not fail the people of East Timor and called for the end of violence.

On 31 August, a letter was sent to Ian Martin, the head of UNAMET during the period of the count, by UNIF (the umbrella organisation representing the pro-Indonesian side) lodging a complaint about the ballot. The letter was signed by a presidium of four including Lopes Da C'ruz, Indonesia's Ambassador at Large for East Timor. There were seven specific complaints listed.

> On one side, we can see how responsive the Timorese are to decide their own future. On the other, however, we can see how the UNAMET personnel had abused the trust of the voters by conducting acts beyond the mandate of an electoral officer by trying to lead voters to choose a specific option, and by misleading, forcing, intimidating, terrorising.
>
> The act of the electoral section to reject the names of party agents that were submitted by UNIF and the rejection of an open discussion regarding the site of the counting of the ballot, all of which happened at the last minutes of the holding of the ballot, had ruined all our trust and willingness to cooperate with UNAMET, since we are not involved at all directly in the process of the ballot.
>
> With the absence of UNIF's party agent at the polling stations, it is very difficult to observe the process directly in order to give an overall assessment and judgement in relation to the justness, fairness and legitimacy of the ballot itself.

The absence of the party agents has also affected the process taking place at the polling stations, because there is no witness from both sides to check whether the ballot boxes are empty, the booths are safe, the ballot boxes are secure and trustworthy, the UNAMET personnel are not persuading people to choose a certain option and another thousands of things that need to be watched by the party agents to prove the justness, fairness and legitimacy of the process.

There are still too many deficiencies. First, the booths that are made of simple and cheap materials that look like toy boxes for baby games which is not convenient at all for the voter to feel at ease, free and secure to make a choice. Second, the ballot boxes that look like a simple plastic bucket with an opening that may allow any people to insert a hand and change all the ballot papers. Third, the availability of the number of the ballot papers with more than the registered voters which may lead to a manipulation in the replacement of all the marked ballot papers if the choice is not in compliance with the desire of the UNAMET staff present. Fourth, the number of voters that exceed the list of registered voters. Fifth, the excessive presence around the booth area and at the polling vicinities of more local electoral attendants who are mostly from the CNRT members may, psychologically, put an indirect pressure on the voters who want to make a choice. Sixth, the presence of foreign unofficial individuals trying to persuade the voters to choose one option. Seventh, the tendency of some UNAMET individuals trying to steal the opportunity to use its influence and power to lead the voters to choose one option, namely CNRT.

. . . all the above cases have made the balloting process meaningless, not legitimate, unfair, unjust and not transparent at all.

I first saw the letter back in Canberra, a few days after the results had been announced. I carefully considered its contents and concluded I had seen nothing at the many polling places I visited that would give legitimacy to the complaints. Among other things, it would have been simply impossible to insert even the smallest hand into the ballot box and change the ballot papers. I learnt from various sources that the Indonesian Cabinet had subsequently discussed the propriety and integrity of the ballot, and it concluded that even if the allegations had any substance, the overall result would not have changed because at the most the ballot would have been affected by one or two percentage points.

So, at last, and slightly ahead of schedule, the result was out and reported around the world and through the militia camps of East Timor. The very clear-cut vote in favour of independence sadly became the provocation for weeks of brutality and destruction in many parts of East Timor. The announcement of the ballot result was the signal the militia had been waiting for to wreak their havoc.

The last formal task required of the delegation was to report to the Minister for Foreign Affairs, Alexander Downer. I met with Alexander in his first floor Parliament House office on Thursday 2 September, and after a few minutes of private conversation we were joined by some of my delegation colleagues. We explained to the Minister how volatile the security situation had been, but emphasised that the ballot was conducted fairly and freely. We referred to the good work of many, including the UNAMET team, the military liaison officers' unit and CIVPOL.

Minister Downer thanked the delegation for its work and I arranged for some additional thank you letters to be sent to those who had helped the delegation. I thought to myself, 'Job done, it is now over to others to implement the clear-cut result'.

The delegation's formal report was tabled in the House of Representatives about two weeks later. It read in part:

> The Delegation received a consistent message that widespread intimidation of pro-independence supporters had occurred and was continuing to occur in East Timor. Many independence supporters had been forced to leave their homes, some had fled to the hills and others were IDPs (internally displaced people) in the larger towns. There was also a pervasive atmosphere of rumour and threats about what would happen after the poll if voters chose independence. There was clear evidence that the election campaign had not taken place on an even playing field, for example CNRT had not been able to campaign at all in Liquica. However, the East Timorese people were determined to exercise their right to vote and all Delegation interlocutors believed that electoral education from both UNAMET and private sources had been sufficient to provide most people with information on how to vote. UNAMET's technical arrangement for the poll were obviously excellent.

A short formal statement from the delegation was included in the report.

> After visiting Dili, Balibo, Liquica, and Maliana on election day the Australian Observer Delegation has concluded that, within these polling places, procedures allowed for a vote which was secret, free and fair.
>   The sight of thousands of East Timorese waiting to vote with their registration cards in hand at the opening of the polling places gave the day a flying

start against the odds and the East Timorese people are to be congratulated for their courage and determination.

There is no doubt that the technical side of the poll including ballot box procedure went well under the rigorous UNAMET procedures.

The UNAMET leadership and its teams throughout East Timor deserve congratulations on overcoming the major logistical problems covering the many isolated communities in East Timor.

The Delegation also congratulated CIVPOL and the Indonesian Police for outstanding work on the day, particularly in Liquica.

The Delegation added that the implementation phase of the decision of the East Timorese people, whatever it might be, would require an equally determined commitment by those involved.

The security situation was very much part of the delegation's deliberations both as it related to our own protection while we were in East Timor, and in terms of what would happen next. While the consequences of the ballot result was formally outside our brief, we did make reference to our concerns in the closing paragraphs of our report.

It is of great concern that throughout 31 August there were reports of violence in several areas of East Timor by the members of the various pro-integration militia. These include attacks on local staff members of UNAMET.

The Delegation concluded that at the polling stations which it observed, East Timorese were able to exercise a free vote. However, this remarkable achievement must be followed up by a commitment to the result of the Consultation by all the people of East Timor. It urges the Australian Government to continue to assist UNAMET and the people of East Timor achieve a peaceful outcome and reconciliation.

The Delegation wishes to thank all its interlocutors in East Timor. They gave of their time and experience most generously and enabled the Delegation to carry out its responsibilities.

The Delegation also wishes to thank DFAT and ADF staff from the Australian Embassy in Jakarta and the Consulate in Dili for the excellent program arrangements and their unflagging support in all areas of the Delegation's activities. The Delegation also thanks members of the Australian Federal Police and POLRI for the provision of security.

As both Houses of Parliament were sitting on that first Thursday morning back in Canberra, I took the opportunity to make a personal explanation about the '60 Minutes' saga on the floor of the House of Representatives. Once again, I set out the facts and was supported by the Shadow Minister, Laurie Brereton, who explained how he and Marise Payne had been subject to intense intimidation at roadblocks around Liquica. He addressed the House:

As a member of the delegation which was so outstandingly led by the member for Farrer, it is appropriate that I should make some remarks. Whilst I was not part of the convoy that Richard Carleton was following around, which was Mr Fischer's convoy, I had gone to another part of the island across in the west, Maliana, and had to return that afternoon through Liquica, the area where the Carleton incident occurred. In the whole of the day it was the only security problem that we faced directly, in that roadblocks were established after the incident and Senator Payne and I were forced to run the gauntlet of those.

Our great concern was for the many journalists and international observers who had to travel that road later on in the afternoon without the benefit of the police escorts that were afforded to us. It was an incident that marred an otherwise enormously successful Australian contribution to election day observers, journalists and the parliamentary delegation itself, and it is extremely regrettable that Richard Carleton and these antics turned what was an enormously important event in East Timor into a media circus back at home.

A few days after this clarification for the Parliament, we learnt of more trouble around Liquica when Earl Candler, a US citizen working for CIVPOL, had been fired on by militia and Kopassus forces. Kopassus, the elite special forces command unit with strength of around 6000 soldiers, was responsible for Indonesian para-commando operations including unconventional warfare and counter/antiterrorist operations. The relationship between the Kopassus and the militia has become increasingly apparent with time and will, no doubt, be the subject of long debate and deliberation. There is mounting evidence that Kopassus was not controlled on the ground in East Timor.

Specific evidence about Kopassus's involvement emerged when one of its commanders gave evidence to the Indonesian Commission of Inquiry that he had been trained as a militia leader by a Kopassus unit and that Kopassus officers ordered him to kill eight people after the ballot took place. The Indonesian Commission of Inquiry has a huge job in getting to the bottom of the relationship between the Indonesian Army, Kopassus and the militia.

In the few short months since the ballot, intelligence reports have also pointed the finger at who was to blame for the militia carnage. I am not in a position to confirm or reject the veracity of the intelligence reports received by the Australian Government, but I have sifted through information on the public record and two key issues have emerged in relation to Indonesia's tactics.

The first is the existence of a plan to create mayhem if the vote was pro-independence. This plan appears to have been driven by a combination of revenge, as a warning call to other volatile parts of Indonesia and obscure politicking for the Indonesian presidency. It all got out of hand, even in the eyes of the generals in the Indonesian Army, and the cost in loss of life has been horrific. The second issue relates to Indonesia's strategy of greatly weakening East Timor's population. If East Timor was to be independent, then the ranks of independence supporters would be slashed by the wave of militia killing.

A very large cross must go against the Indonesian Army, the police and Kopassus who clearly had in place a strategy to pursue a scorched-earth policy in the event of a vote for independence. With the exception of Baucau (where the relationship between church leaders and the militia was strong enough to make a difference), this policy applied across the whole of East Timor. A second cross against the Indonesians relates to timing. Haste and lack of planning on Indonesia's part in the lead up to the ballot meant that there was no time to prepare a comprehensive set of options in the event of either an autonomy or independence vote.

Notwithstanding all of the death and destruction, I think Indonesia does deserve a number of ticks. President Habibie did deliver on his word. Indonesia approved the conduct of a ballot for self-determination, and more quickly than originally envisaged. In addition, with the eyes of the world upon him, President Habibie confronted the growing mayhem and had the courage to say that if the Indonesian police and army were unable to establish control in East Timor, he would agree to have armed international peace-makers and peace-keepers on the ground. President Habibie also came through on the night of 19 October when, at around midnight, the People's Consultative Assembly affirmed the result of the ballot and voted to revoke Indonesian sovereignty over East Timor thus paving the way for the creation of the independent nation of East Timor.

The president's role requires detailed analysis down the track, but clearly he was not under any illusions as to what would happen if the ballot result were to be in favour of independence. Sir Leon Brittan, Senior European Commissioner, visited Jakarta in early April 1999 and, among other things, raised concerns over militia violence in East Timor and the possible role of former President Soeharto. Clearly President Habibie was aware of deep-seated international doubts about security even in April.

On the day the delegation departed East Timor, security began to deteriorate rapidly. UN staff and journalists came under fire at the main UN compound in Dili. In many distant parts of East Timor a pattern that would become all too familiar emerged. Local POLRI would suddenly pronounce they could no longer guarantee the security of UN personnel and advised that there should be an immediate withdrawal. Gunfire, direct and indirect, would continue until all UN personnel left. In Liquica on 4 September a full-scale assault was launched by the militia on UNAMET within seven hours of the announcement of the ballot result. A UN vehicle was hit by gunshot eighteen times and Earl Candler wounded. A touch and go evacuation involving Paul Mulqueeney and the remaining team took place. UNAMET was never to return to Liquica.

The death and injury count mounted rapidly and

the withdrawals were followed by the wanton destruction of buildings. Bishop Belo was evacuated on 7 September and his main residence was burnt to the ground shortly afterwards.

The worst period of violence, however, occurred between 8 and 20 September. During these twelve days, the Australian Army's Colonel Ken Brownrigg and Captain Noel Henderson maintained the Australian Consulate compound with a handful of UNAMET personnel; everybody else had been evacuated. Unarmed and with help a long way away, the only thing between them and a full on attack by rampaging militia, particularly if using bulldozers, were the high walls topped with barbed wire. Top marks to these two unsung heroes.

Those responsible for the violence, however senior or junior, will have to live with their conscience and the ugly postscript they created.

Before departing Canberra after the House adjourned, I returned to my desk to get stuck into the electorate work that had piled up while I was away. I was very happy to be heading home, where once again my wife Judy had been very supportive handling so many things during my absence.

My selection as delegation leader had been completely unexpected, but it turned out to be an extraordinary and astonishingly worthwhile experience. I'm under no illusions that what we did was anything other than a very tiny part of the whole process. It is now over to the UN and to INTERFET, the Australian and Indonesian governments, together with the Government of Portugal, to push forward the decision taken by the people of East Timor on 30 August 1999.

TEN

THE MEDIA MAYHEM

THE ROLE OF the media through the entire East Timor ballot process deserves some examination and should be put in historical context. No doubt the analysis and debate will continue for years.

The twentieth century began with the first-ever detailed media coverage of warfare during the Boer War. Among the prominent journalists covering that conflict was Winston Churchill. He was but one of many whose reporting was crucial to Britain's conduct of hostilities, something General Kitchener, placed in overall control of the war, was well aware of. When, at one point, a breakthrough was needed to maintain momentum and popular support for the war, reporting of the Relief of Mafeking became required reading in the United Kingdom. Daily, the public pored over dramatic accounts in the press, sent by telegram from journalists 'on the ground' in distant South Africa.

This was the beginning of the close relationship

between war and 'instant news'. But the press's role has many aspects. After World War I, American journalist, Lowell Thomas, elevated Colonel T. E. Lawrence to Lawrence of Arabia, the hero in white robes who united the Arabs and liberated Damascus. Thomas's version of events conveniently ignored the fact that Australian diggers, led by the brilliant General Harry Chauvel, captured Damascus two days before the arrival of the British (led by General Allenby), Lawrence and the press. The dramatic media report is not always accurate.

World War II saw radio and the movies used for the first time to provide news—and often propaganda. And, in the case of radio, coded messages were regularly sent after the main evening news broadcasts, to resistance fighters across Europe.

Television reporting (and blockbuster treatment by Hollywood) occurred first during the Korean War and then more so during the war in Vietnam. The fact that TV reporters seemed to be everywhere in Vietnam added, in the later stages of war, to the steady growth of criticism of the strategies adopted and eventually placed the purpose of the war under direct question. From my own experience in Vietnam, with the Australia Task Force in Phuoc Tuy Province, it was clear that the role of the media became a factor at an operational level as well as at the broader strategic level.

Intensity of media coverage reached its height during the Gulf War. The war was brought into everyone's lounge rooms by the famous CNN reports, live from Baghdad as the salvos of US missiles slammed into that city. Missile targets and the moment of impact by 'smart bombs' were captured by video cameras in real time, in a way World War II tacticians and Bomber Command could only dream about.

Now move forward to Bosnia, Kosovo and East Timor.

In these irregular conflicts, the media seemed prepared to risk a great deal, even their own lives, to get the extra footage in circumstances where the 'front line' was constantly changing or non-existent. In Kosovo, radio broadcasters were greatly assisted by the advent of good mobile telephone coverage. Furthermore, during hostilities in Serbia, Western journalists had direct on-the-spot access to the rest of the world using satellite links through networks such as CNN. East Timor saw all of this replicated, with state-of-the-art TV cameras, satellite equipment, mobile telephones and good old-fashioned photography of the highest quality.

After the Howard to Habibie letter on East Timor was leaked in mid-January 1999, many Australian and international journalists resumed travelling to Indonesia and to East Timor. They were quick to sense a developing story. Some of them, with years of experience in Asian theatres of war, were ready to take calculated risks to get the story of the day and the week.

As always, the media on the ground fell into a number of loose groupings—the fundamental split was between the print media and the radio/TV journalists and their crews. There was also a further split between those who had been on the case for a relatively long time (the 'long-stay, live in Dili' category) and those who saw the story as a short-term assignment (the 'fly-in' category who whipped in, gathered as many stories as they could over one or two days and whipped out again to Bali or beyond). As interest in East Timor grew throughout July and August, journalists in both categories began to file many stories back to their headquarters and, increasingly, found the take-up rate very satisfactory.

The media in East Timor, by and large, did an excellent job during the ballot period and in its immediate aftermath. Many worked very hard and travelled well past Dili to report from hotspots such as Maliana in the west and Baucau and beyond in the east. They were able to get a sense of how fragile the situation was away from Dili itself.

The concerns of the international media in the days leading up to the poll were threefold. First, there was a strong feeling that the militia (with the tacit consent of the Indonesian Army) would go berserk and orchestrate a mini-holocaust in the event of a clear-cut result in favour of independence. Second, most wanted to ensure that their own staff, be that driver or crew, would be given evacuation assistance, unlike what happened in Vietnam. I was impressed by this genuineness in seeking to look after those East Timorese and Indonesians who had compromised themselves in the eyes of the militia by working with and being paid by the Western media. Third, and not unnaturally, these journalists on the ground in East Timor were concerned about their own skins and the prospect that they might not get out alive, especially if the descent into mayhem occurred suddenly.

This third fear became a reality on Tuesday 21 September when a young Dutch journalist, Sander Thoenes, turned the wrong way on departure from the Hotel Turismo to be slaughtered less than an hour later. Sander was a dedicated multi-lingual journalist experienced in reporting from many difficult places. He was on duty for the *Financial Times* when his luck ran out. The full circumstances of his murder are yet to be determined, but my suspicion is a simple one—he was judged to be an Australian, and therefore an appropriate target.

It was a very risky business being a member of the media on the ground in East Timor. The sometimes minimal security provided by the Indonesian Army and Indonesian Police to UNAMET personnel under agreed security guidelines was not automatically extended to the representatives of the world's press. They had to take their chances like any other resident of East Timor. Despite all of these difficulties, I found the coverage provided from East Timor, by and large, to be accurate and balanced, particularly during the period of my stay. It was extremely helpful to have the observations of the delegation backed up by extensive media reports showing the East Timorese stepping up in large numbers to vote despite the potential for violence.

It was equally important to have the media cover the 'machinery' of the ballot, including the collection of the ballot boxes and the counting procedure. This added authenticity to the reports and the statements of the observer delegations from around the world that the ballot had been secret, free and fair.

In giving the thumbs up to the media on the ground in East Timor, I do so with the exception of Richard Carleton. On 8 September, I lodged a formal complaint about the incidents at Liquica and related matters with David Leckie, Managing Director and Chief Executive Officer of the Nine Network. I wrote:

> It is my desire to formally lodge with you a complaint in relation to the conduct of Richard Carleton of 60 Minutes and the 60 Minutes program as detailed forthwith.
>
> On Monday, 30 August, Richard Carleton persisted interviewing a militia leader, with particularly direct questioning, to a point which resulted in a flare up with the militia at Liquica. This in turn endangered the lives of the 60 Minutes team and other personnel in Liquica, including UNAMET and CIVPOL personnel.
>
> In relation to this, I would point out that at the time Richard Carleton recorded the two interviews with me at the first and second polling places at

Liquica, I was not aware of his intense interview directly with a member of the militia, part of which 60 Minutes showed on Sunday night. Even from the short extract of this interview it was obvious that the militia was being provoked in a situation where there was every reason to have deep-seated concern about the ramifications of that provocation.

The interview conduct by Richard Carleton was in breach of UNAMET rules, both in relation to interviewing voters, as well as a member or members of the militia. My objection has intensified as more information has become available, but even in Richard Carleton's direct interview with me I was expressing concern and caution. I submit on this, his conduct was not good journalism but reckless and irresponsible.

Richard Carleton subsequently had to be rescued from the Liquica Police Station where inside the leader of the local militia was dominating proceedings and carrying out a very direct interview with Richard Carleton. What was not made clear, and may not be known to you, is that part of the deal to extract Richard Carleton and his team from Liquica Police Station and away from the Liquica militia, was that we would upon return to Dili proceed to the Dili Police Station where the whole matter could be sorted out.

I may well have been delivering Richard Carleton into custody at the Dili Police Station, to quote Richard's snide comment to air, but the point might well be made in the interest of fair play, that I was delivering him out of custody of the Liquica based police and militia. I would seek acknowledgment of this aspect.

60 Minutes kindly agreed to obscure the faces of the voters being directly interviewed by Richard Carleton contrary to UNAMET rules, but for some reason or other the particular pixellation really was

inadequate. It could easily allow for identification in circumstances which remain both brutal and fragile and could also lead to the death of those East Timorese voters being interviewed directly by Richard Carleton and asked how they were going to vote. Was there a reason not to go the full process to ensure absolute cover of the faces of those voters?

I know that you have given consideration to these matters already. I would invite you to write to me when convenient in respect of the above three aspects.

I remain absolutely of the view that Richard Carleton not only put his life at risk, as he himself stated, but unnecessarily put other lives at risk.

I look forward to hearing from you.

On 23 September I received a reply from David Leckie.

Thank you for your letter of September 8th regarding Richard Carleton's recent assignment in East Timor. The Network values, and I personally value, the views of anyone as experienced and knowledgeable as yourself. Accordingly we take very seriously your assessment of the conduct of Carleton and the 60 Minutes crew.

Carleton had not registered with UNAMET and therefore, strictly speaking, he was not bound by their guidelines in his reporting. He tells me he had planned to register in due course but he had been in Timor 26 hours at the time trouble erupted. He worked on Sunday evening and again from 6.00 am on polling day. He says the 'formalities' of registration would have come later.

Nevertheless this really begs the question whether he was right or wrong to ask voters their voting intentions.

In his defence, Carleton has shown me an array of

newspaper reports that clearly identify (sometimes with photos) individuals and how they voted or intended to vote. The reporters, some of the most experienced in Asia, were presumably registered with UNAMET. The newspapers include *The New York Times*, *The Washington Post*, *Los Angeles Times*, *International Herald Tribune*, *The Sydney Morning Herald* and *The Age*. No doubt there are others. I also heard Graham Richardson comment on radio 2GB that there was no point in covering an election if you were not going to ask how people were going to vote.

So on balance, I am of the view that Carleton was right to ask about voting intentions and we were right to obscure faces.

The attempted interview with the militiaman occurred spontaneously as the report to air shows. I simply cannot agree that this was done with intent to be reckless or irresponsible.

The questions that arises from this incident is whether what ensued could have been predicted. It is Carleton's view that it was not the interview attempt that upset the militiaman but rather the crowd's laughter. This laughter was not predictable.

Carleton has reported wars and civil disturbances in Lebanon, Jordan, Iraq, West Bank, Gaza, Syria, Saudi Arabia, Afghanistan, Namibia, Angola, Congo (formerly Zaire), Conga (Brazzaville), Eritrea, South Africa, the then Rhodesia, Algeria, Liberia, Bosnia, Croatia, Serbia, Kosovo, Cyprus, Azerbaijan, Vietnam, Cambodia and elsewhere. With this experience, I have to rely on his judgement when he is on the ground.

With the benefit of hindsight of course everyone would wish that the Timor incident had not occurred. Nor is it an incident I would like to see repeated. But I believe any suggestion that it was intentionally caused is false.

Your role in extricating the crew from the Liquica Police Station is acknowledged and appreciated. However, I am informed that the deal you struck was done without any reference to Carleton or the crew. It was not until the drive back to Dili that Carleton was told you were taking him to Dili police.

Carleton readily acknowledges that in taking his camera tapes you were acting in good faith and with intent to help. However, again with hindsight, it was a somewhat dangerous thing to do. It could have compromised the independence of your delegation and it may still be used by the Indonesians as 'evidence' of partiality. Further, had Dili police required Carleton to produce the tapes, as they well might, the fact that he could not would surely have been seen by the police as evidence of Carleton's 'guilty intent'.

The pixellation we used in the story, whilst it was subtle, was certainly adequate.

I would like to assure you that I consider this incident to be of the utmost concern. It has been the subject of intense discussion, investigation and soul searching. For 21 years, 60 Minute reports [sic] and crews have filmed in war zones and the trouble spots of the globe with bravery and dedication. Some of these assignments have been difficult and at times downright dangerous. It is to the credit and good judgement of the teams that they are all still with us today.

You'll note that in his reply, David Leckie conceded that Richard Carleton had not registered with UNAMET. Carleton has also acknowledged that he was in East Timor on an incorrect visa. On the issue of the direct questions about voting intent, David Leckie used photos published in *The New York Times*, the *Age* and other newspapers in Richard Carleton's defence. In the main, these photos were taken during the election campaign, which is quite different to interviewing voters about their intentions in full view of local militia. This was, of course, in direct breach of UNAMET regulations issued prior to polling day. (UNAMET notifications 9, 14 and 20, which combined with other requirements, directly procluded questions about voting intent being asked of voters in front of polling places.) Leckie is correct that the rules are addressed to registered journalists and delegations, and that Carleton had not registered. He may well be correct, also, that there was no deliberate intention to be reckless or irresponsible. I had not suggested that.

I remain of the view that these interviews were reckless and irresponsible, and could have endangered the lives of those being interviewed. The possibility of disruption to the ballot was heightened as was the chance of ensuing violence. Indeed, it was a few days later that American CIVPOL worker Earl Candler was shot in the stomach at Liquica.

My third area of concern related to the interview with a member of the militia. When '60 Minutes' put the segment to air, it was clear that the militia leader was upset by Richard Carleton's intervention. The argument that the crowd's laughter provoked the militiaman does not ring true for a journalist as experienced as Richard Carleton. There is one golden rule in Asia and that is never place anyone in a situation of direct 'loss of face'. Inevitably, there will be consequences, and even Channel 9 concedes that the militia leader was put in such a position.

Now, of course, many around the world would say 'so what?'. Given their appalling behaviour, the militia should have been made to experience 'loss of face' (or worse) at every opportunity. But this is not a relevant point when the objective on polling day was to keep the situation calm, and to allow as many people as possible to vote.

Carleton would later defend his decisions, saying that there had been no time to get the right visa, and that other journalists also used tourist visas; that he had done no more to identify pro-independence voters than many of them did themselves, by celebrating openly on the streets of Dili; and that the militia leader deserved to be questioned directly and forcefully, because of past acts of violence. None of those responses changes my opinion. I have no particular ongoing beef with Richard Carleton. I have stated these events as they unfolded and it is now a case of moving on.

Perhaps I am too close to the whole saga to be objective and to make a final judgement. Rather, I leave this to those who wrote to '60 Minutes' after the full report was screened on 5 September. On Sunday 12 September the program aired a summary of these letters. This was 'new age sensitive' television with Richard Carleton admitting direct to camera that '60 Minutes' had received many letters relating to the East Timor segment and that three-quarters of these went against the report. However, the real crunch had been delivered by ABC TV's 'Media Watch' on Monday 6 September. Presenter Richard Ackland tore apart Richard Carleton's story, highlighting amongst other things that Lieutenant Arly had been part of the Australian delegation's security detail and that he had helped defuse a particularly critical (and unnecessary) situation.

I caught up with Richard Carleton's astonishing admission that the letters had gone against him whilst en route to a four-day break in the Carnarvon Gorge in central Queensland with Judy and the boys. It provided a delicious start to the bushwalking holiday, but not one I felt triumphant about. Whilst I was tempted to say 'game, set and match to Fischer', all in all the whole saga was something the Australian Consulate team and the Australian cause could have done well without. Above all else, the hard-pressed UNAMET and CIVPOL team on the ground at Liquica needed this flare up like a hole in the head or a kick in the stomach.

Reporting and media comment from Australia, Indonesia, the USA and elsewhere on the whole East Timor situation showed that the broad Left and the 'hindsight revisionists' were well and truly out and about in large numbers. In Australia, the media simply could not get used to a 'right-wing' Government led by a conservative prime minister, John Howard, pushing ahead on East Timor in a way that Labor had failed to do under Hawke and Keating as prime ministers, or Bill Hayden and Gareth Evans as foreign ministers. Both John Howard and Alexander Downer, drove forward the issue with the letter in 1998 and followed up with determined activity throughout the first eight months of 1999. This, and the barely concealed surprise in some sections of the media, coloured some of the reporting and commentary, but nothing could take away from the fact that in 1999 the people of East Timor were voting on real options. Five years ago, no one would have predicted that an Indonesian-agreed ballot would be taking place just as no one would have predicted in 1984 that the Berlin Wall would come crashing down five years later.

The most alarming feature of media reaction was the emergence of 20/20 hindsight from commentators who pronounced as though they knew all along what should have happened. First, it was said, Howard should not have written his letter, as it was clearly premature to impose such proposals on a weakened president and a weakened Indonesia. The short answer to this is that it was always Indonesia's call to decide exactly when, or even if, a ballot would be held. Had Habibie wanted to, the gently expressed proposal in John Howard's letter could have been rejected by the president, whether he was weakened or not.

The 'hindsight revisionists', having said it was too early to propose a ballot, then said it would be absurd to proceed with the ballot without having armed peace-makers or peace-keepers on the ground before polling day. The sad but direct answer to this is that it is clear Indonesia would not have allowed the ballot to proceed at all under those conditions. Article 3 of the agreement establishing the ballot process spelt out that Indonesia had responsibility for providing the security. Several attempts by Australia and other interlocutors to change this did not succeed.

Some in the media said that UNAMET should have known better, and should have acted pre-emptively on various intelligence reports regarding the build-up of the militia. The capacity of UNAMET, unarmed as it was, to successfully manage a 'full on' confrontation in the media and with the militia was extremely limited. If UNAMET had reacted as some in the media demanded, it would have probably led to a collapse of the preparations for registration and the conduct of the ballot on 30 August.

The final claim by the hindsight specialists was that Australia should have gone into East Timor with armed forces within 24 hours of the announcement of the result on Sunday 5 September. As the Prime Minister correctly contended, to go in without the clearance of the Indonesians was tantamount to a declaration of war between Australia and Indonesia. It was simply not on.

In rejecting these claims, I am not providing a knee-jerk defence of either Australian policy or the UNAMET approach. I contend that the media, its sometimes far too shrill comments and its need for dramatic coverage (as if militia activity needed any more drama), simply ignored the circumstances and what was realistic and possible.

There is no doubt that the stakes were high for both East Timor and Indonesia. The situation was complex and the week we were in East Timor proved to be a decisive turning point for national sovereignty. No media criticism can take away from the fact that the East Timorese did vote and voted for independence. Whilst it will take some time to come to terms with the full consequences of this, the clear-cut result cannot be ignored by the media, by the governments of the world or by the UN.

At least in East Timor in 1999, we were spared headlines such as 'GOTCHA', which appeared in the English tabloids after the British sank the Argentine ship, *Belgrano* during the Falklands War in 1982. This is a significant point as context is very important. A photograph of an Australian soldier pointing a gun at an East Timorese (probably a member of the militia) lying spread-eagled on the ground and blindfolded, created considerable difficulties when printed without any explanation in the Indonesian press.

These difficulties, however, are small compared to all those that have to be overcome in rebuilding the relationship between Australia and Indonesia. With the help of balanced media, this is an achievable task that will be helped by resumed growth in trade, investment and tourism links a little way down the track. And, all things considered, the media were very helpful in proving to the world that East Timor had voted, in verifying the clear-cut result and in bringing home that the agony on the new island state had to be dealt with as quickly as possible.

My own relationships with the media generally, specific journalists, and some of the media moguls in particular, has fluctuated wildly over my time in politics.

Throughout my decade as National Party leader, I gained invaluable experience in how to get it right and how to get it wrong from my daily dealings with the media and this helped a great deal in my work with the Australian Observer Delegation.

I've been reasonably open, available and proactive, initiating contact quickly when there was a fast-breaking story of one kind or another. My favourite medium has always been ABC morning radio with its powerful reach across country Australia. Radio provides great flexibility so long as you have a clear telephone line or mobile telephone connection. Mind you, I was somewhat embarrassed when in the middle of a live interview with John Laws to announce Telstra's decision to replace the analogue mobile network with the CDMA digital network, my mobile phone connection dropped out.

Over the years I have been even more embarrassed by sometimes overdoing it when contacting columns such as 'Stay in Touch' in the *Sydney Morning Herald* and 'Melba' in *The Australian* with colour items which, on occasions, were twisted and used against me. As a result, my media staff imposed an absolute rule (with rolling extensions) banning me from ringing any columns for at least twelve months. This rule applied throughout my whole time as Deputy Prime Minister. I was also subjected to 'rule seven': if I rang a radio station early in the morning with a news grab, I had to let my hardworking press secretaries know as soon as possible that I had done so. After a period in government, I found myself more guarded but able to handle print media and radio, I think, quite successfully. I had less success with the difficult medium of television.

I used all of these skills to avoid any loose comments that might have caused diplomatic problems during my days in East Timor. I did as much radio as possible, particularly back to the electorate and used the opportunity to explain why regional stability in nearby Asia was important for all of Australia.

In all my interviews from East Timor and in the immediate period after I returned, I confess I unashamedly sought to add to the profile of our key findings and to build a case that would withstand any eleventh hour attempt by hardliners within Indonesia to destroy the integrity of the ballot. Despite an occasional grumble and an obvious exception, the media in East Timor, especially during the period of the ballot, helped in this task. They provided a valuable service and maintained high standards in very challenging circumstances. And the world should be grateful for the high-risk effort put in by front-line media.

ELEVEN

THE FUTURE

As WE CONSIDER East Timor's future, it is interesting to examine its economic prospects by looking, in part, at the performance of other tiny nations in and around Asia. Believe it or not, in terms of landmass, East Timor is nine times larger than Mauritius, nineteen times larger than Singapore, and about half the size of Bhutan. Its population is about equal to Bhutan, slightly smaller than Mauritius and a good deal smaller than Singapore.

I accept the need to be very cautious in making comparisons and in drawing conclusions about East Timor's prospects for two good reasons. First, it is just too early to know how quickly progress will be made in rebuilding the economy. Second, the very unlevel playing field of international trade is probably going to become even more uneven after the breakdown in negotiations at the December 1999 ministerial meeting of the World Trade Organization in Seattle. Nevertheless, I will chance my arm by looking at how successful a number of small nations have been in developing their economies and how they might be an example for East Timor.

As the tiny nation-state of East Timor emerges from the extraordinary events of 1999, it faces a bright, not a bleak, future. In recent decades, the world has seen new nation-states successfully carve out niches for themselves where the description 'small' has become a strength, not a weakness. This can certainly happen in East Timor with its land area of less than 1500 square kilometres and population of less than one million. East Timor only needs to look to Bhutan and Singapore or Mauritius for a model.

Land-bound Bhutan is squeezed between Nepal and the giants of India and China. With a population of around one million, a form of constitutional monarchy and a degree of hegemony with India, it is carefully modernising, but without losing its core culture. Rigid controls on tourism are helping, even though this Shangri-la in the Himalayas is not without some problems. In Southern Bhutan there has been considerable violence involving local residents of Nepali descent, many of whom have left to live in refugee camps in Nepal. The governments of Bhutan and Nepal have resolved to try and find a solution to the problem and a way around their differences. Nevertheless, Bhutan is not bankrupt and continues to boost economic growth and health and education standards through major hydro-electricity projects and primary industry development.

The Republic of Singapore has the advantage of its unique strategic location on the major sea lanes and air corridors of the world. With a population of around four million, it is one of the leading economies of Southeast Asia, and has benefited greatly from tourism, but even more so from the development of its port. The first quarter of the twenty-first century will see Singapore emerge, with Rotterdam and Los Angeles, as just one of a handful of super hub ports of world shipping.

Mauritius is showing the way with the development of small island tourism. This has been linked to a push to establish itself as a stopover place on an alternative route between Australia and Europe.

And now, the tiny nation-state of East Timor has arrived new on the Asian stage. Entering from stage left, it will, in due course, become a member of the Association of South-East Asian Nations (ASEAN), and further down the track the Asia Pacific Economic Cooperation organisation (APEC). In some ways it will fit easily between the example provided by Bhutan, with its cottage economy backed by giant hydro-electric projects, and that of Singapore, with its large-scale tourism and hub transport role.

East Timor has enormous potential to develop in a sensitive and environmentally-friendly way. The world's middle-classes have an insatiable appetite for tourism, so long as safety and security can be guaranteed. East Timor will rate well as an adventure tourism destination with its corridor of fine beaches, verdant mountain scenery and excellent climate, particularly from April through to October. If the famous statue of Jesus Christ survives and is reorientated away from Jakarta and rededicated, East Timor could also become a place of Easter pilgrimage for southern hemisphere Christians.

Blending the best of Bhutan, Singapore and Mauritius will provide a helpful guide to the development of tourism. However, tourism alone cannot drive forward East Timor's economy. Natural resources such as marble, and oil and gas (from the Timor Gap) are available and plentiful, and represent enormous potential for big project development with guaranteed revenue streams. As a bonus, East Timor could quickly recover its coffee and tea plantations and other agricultural resources making a feature of their organic production. The Gleno area is one part of East Timor that has real potential in this regard, but will need a great deal of help.

The question is whether East Timor is so small that it simply will not be able to break through in a very uneven international economic, trade, investment and tourism environment. Again, implementing the very best aspects of Bhutan and Singapore will help. However, East Timor has an additional and unique support network, that of the Catholic Church.

The Catholic Church in Portugal and Australia has a longstanding commitment to the people of East Timor. Its worldwide networks are of great strength and should be made to work towards rebuilding the tiny nation-state, especially in its first decade, much in the same way the international Zionist movement supported the modernisation and expansion of the Israeli economy.

The key to early success in the redevelopment of East Timor will be its relationship with its giant neighbours of Indonesia and Australia. Significantly, in the aftermath of the ballot, senior figures in all three countries strongly referred to this. What is needed, of course, is more than words, more than rhetoric and symbolic gestures such as visits and revamped aid programs, but action on the ground.

The irony is that the sometimes destructive elements of centralisation, combined with the enlightened aspects of globalisation, can work to create improved prospects for the development of niche markets, especially with the opportunities provided by the Internet and electronic commerce. The brilliant fabric weavings of East Timor could be marketed, for example, in a way similar to that of the Northern Territory's 'Micks Whips'. Mick

Denigan, who lives at Howard Springs, south of Darwin, is selling his hand-platted whips and belts made from Northern Territory cattle and crocodile hides to the world. Since establishing his Web page two years ago, orders have flooded in by e-mail to such an extent that he now employs eight people. The same opportunities await the creative people of East Timor.

Cottage economic activity will, of course, have to be backed up by larger scale development, but there are two issues that could wreck recovery if not dealt with. The first is the possibility of violence and disunity destroying prospects for tourism. The second is the chance that East Timor could be over exposed to worldwide economic downturn and the related trend towards trade blocs and isolationism.

Disunity in small nations can be very destructive. In many ways dealing with this will be the most difficult issue confronting the people of East Timor. Many lost parents, brothers, sisters and children at the hands of the militia, East Timorese collaborators and Indonesian provocateurs during the previous quarter of a century. East Timor also has to deal with its more than ten separate ethnic groupings, all of which have their own languages. Within some of the language groups there are also separate dialects (four in Tetum, for example). Each of these groups has a different culture as well.

Counter-balancing these differences is the religious unity of East Timor. Over 90 per cent of the population is Catholic, a legacy of Portuguese colonisation. This in itself does not guarantee unity of purpose, but should be an influence. There are hundreds of churches in East Timor and the majority of these survived the burst of destruction in September 1999, thus providing a physical resource of a kind to help the Church become actively involved in nation building.

Unity of purpose is an essential requirement for the

success of East Timor, the millennium nation-state. If the country's leaders set the example, and are prepared to forgive (though not necessarily forget) and to move the agenda forward as Xanana Gusmao has, then the prospects are bright for the East Timorese and their relationships with one another as well as with Indonesia and Australia.

The second dark cloud on the horizon for East Timor is the prospect of a major economic slowdown in the developed nations of Asia, Europe and the Americas. It is in such circumstances that 'donor fatigue' and the trend to 'look after self' sets in to work against smaller and poorer nations of the world. And, if East Timor borrows heavily it will be even more exposed, as the inevitable slump in oil and gas prices will mean that it will be even less able to service loans. Add to this a wave of corruption in the way some high finance is handled and key projects managed, and you have a recipe for disaster. However, all of this pessimism should be tempered by the fact that in periods of world economic downturn, cottage and small economies sometimes survive with less hurt than larger and more developed nations.

The best way forward is for East Timor to make every effort to avoid the international spivs and snake-oil merchants as well as the worst aspects of aid bureaucracies, such as the huge overhead ratios carried by some of the established world charity funds and the highly paid aid consultants who descend on countries in need. It should aim for moderately-paced economic growth spread across the agriculture and tourism sectors with big ticket development being provided by the oil and gas sectors. A new currency and a new set of stamps will also attract interest and support from the world's cashed-up numismatists. All of this will help build an economic base for East Timor.

Finally, it has to be said that East Timor will not become a new Singapore or Mauritius or Bhutan overnight. The leaders of those countries have worked hard to achieve social cohesion, and economic security. However, with unity of purpose, a good deal of sensible help and a measure of luck, East Timor will be able to gradually rebuild and find a deserved place in the sun after the horrible bloodbath of September 1999.

INTERFET (International Forces East Timor), comprising troops from many countries including Australia, New Zealand and Thailand, has restored security quickly. Against all odds, it has also created a strong basis for the transition from UN administration to a government of the people of East Timor early in the new millennium. Under the leadership of General Peter Cosgrove, INTERFET has had an eye to the future of East Timor by helping rebuild services and infrastructure such as town water supplies.

Some four months after the ballot, as Christmas 1999 loomed, international donor organisations and the World Bank sent representatives to Japan for a special meeting that was attended by Xanana Gusmao. This meeting would test whether or not donor fatigue had set in and if the world was moving on to the next crisis, or if a substantial commitment would be made to rebuilding East Timor. To the surprise of some, the key donor nations doubled expectations and promised over A$800 million to East Timor, with A$100 million coming from Japan and A$25 million from Australia.

When I was asked about this on ABC Radio one Saturday morning, I ventured two reasons for the strong support. The first was that enormous progress had been made on the whole East Timor saga. Indonesia did approve the ballot, the UN agreements were signed, UNAMET was set up, the ballot was conducted and the results declared, Indonesia lifted its sovereignty and security had been restored—all in the calendar year 1999. The template for East Timor's future had been laid down; in the eyes of the donor countries East Timor was a small country that could be efficiently helped and they liked this dimension.

The second reason for such strong international support was an enormous obligation, particularly by Portugal, to the people of East Timor. A token response could have been seen as a breach of faith. There is no doubt that over the previous 24 years many countries had felt similarly obliged and by making a substantial commitment they could not only help speed up East Timor's recovery, but meet their moral obligations as well.

Quick follow-through by donor nations to ensure that aid gets through to Dili and the towns and villages of East Timor will ensure that recovery momentum builds. All in all, it has to be said that the very size of the pledges from international donor countries has provided a very good omen for the future. Whilst there is still a great deal to do, at long last the future is looking better for the people of East Timor.

God bless them all!

INDEX

ABC, 55, 106, 129, 133, 141
Ackland, Richard, 129
Africa, 20–1
Aileu, 58
Aitarak militia, 57
Alatas, Ali, 4, 5–6, 14, 64–5
All Party Delegation, Africa,
  20–1
Allenby, General, 120
Aloud, Matthew, 34
Alvarez, José, 105
Amnesty International, 52
Anderson, David 'Batavia', 36
Anderson, John, 10
Andrews, David, 64
ANFREL, 46
Annan, Kofi A., 4, 38, 109
APEC, 137
Arly, Lieutenant, 61, 72,
  74–5, 89, 104, 129

Army, Indonesian *see*
  Indonesian Army
ASEAN, 137
Asia Pacific Economic
  Cooperation, 137
Asian economic crisis
  (1997–98), 16
Association of South-East
  Asian Nations, 137
Atauro, 102
atrocities, 23, 33
Atsabe, 89, 99–100, 102
Austrade, 3
'Australia All Over' (radio
  program), 55
Australian, 14
Australian Consulate, Dili,
  85–6
Australian Council for
  Overseas Aid, 7

Australian Electoral
  Commission, 8
Australian Federal Police, 20,
  61, 91, 114
Australian Observer
  Delegation: in Baucau and
  Liquica, 32–3; in Gleno,
  43–6; in Liquica, 71–7; in
  Manatuto and Aileu,
  58–60; list of delegates,
  xiii–xiv; polling day,
  66–81; post-poll debriefing,
  82–4; pre-mission briefing,
  4–5; report of, 112–14

Baker, Diane, 44
Balfour, Arthur, 15–16
Balibo, 34, 62, 63, 84
Barisan Rakyat Timor, 37
Barnby, Don, 102
Barreto, Francisco, 88
Batley, James, 22, 50, 76
Baucau, 32, 116
Belgrano (ship), 132
Belo, Bishop Carlos Filipe
  Ximenes, 48–50, 52, 118
Beng Yong Chew, 40
Bhutan, 136
Bidau Santana Primary School,
  66
Boer War, 119
Bong Suk Sohn, 38
Bourne, Vicki, xiii, 6–7, 32,
  67–8, 78, 86, 107
Bowling, Mark, 36
Boyd, Sarah, 54
Bradley, Patrick, 38, 39
Brereton, Laurie: addresses
  Parliament, 114; Fischer
  on, 6; Indonesia refuses
  visa to, 20; member of
  Australian Observer

Delegation, xiii; presents
  Fischer with model steam
  engine, 107; pushes Belo
  on peacekeeping force, 49;
  visits Balibo and Maliana,
  63, 77; visits Falantil
  cantonment, 44; visits
  Liquica, 32; voices security
  concerns, 84
Brittan, Sir Leon, 117
Brownrigg, Ken, 92, 118

Café Bohemia, 36
Calvert, Ashton, 13
Candler, Earl, 115, 117, 128
Caritas, 7, 88
Carleton, Richard, 71–7, 83,
  85, 94–6, 106–7, 114–15,
  123–9
Cartwright, Paul, 20, 62
Castro, Fidel, 56–7
Catholics, 48–50, 138, 139
Channel 9, 93
Chauvel, Harry, 120
Christ, statue of, 19, 96, 97–8
Churchill, Winston, 119
CIVPOL: as security keepers,
  34–5; composition of, 7;
  decides to forgo arms,
  39–40, 62; Fischer
  congratulates, 84; in
  Atsabe, 102; in Gleno, 99,
  101; militia threats to, 55;
  Mills as Chief of, 39
CNN, 26–7, 121
CNRT, 26, 51, 63, 112
Cohen, Barry, 104
Conningham, Kirk, xiii, 7,
  32, 42
Corbett, Wayne, 102
Cosgrove, Peter, 141
Cruz, Lopes Da, 37–8, 109–10

Darwin, 106
Denigan, Mick, 138–9
Department of Foreign Affairs
    and Trade, 2, 4–5, 86
Dili, 19, 22, 67–8
Dili Airport, 105
Dili Beach, 103
Dili massacre, 98–9
Dili Police Station, 74–5
Dowd, John, 52–3
Downer, Alexander: briefs
    Australian delegation, 6; on
    Howard's letter, 14;
    receives Belo's comments
    on ballot, 49; reports to
    Parliament on polling day,
    69–71; retains Foreign
    Affairs portfolio, 10; sounds
    out Fischer as Delegation
    leader, 2; thanks Australian
    delegation, 111; works on
    East Timor issue, 13, 130
Dunn, Jim, 90, 91–2

East Timor: economic
    prospects, 135–40;
    geography, 135; pledges of
    international aid for, 141–2
Electoral Commissioners, 8,
    38–9
Erico, 1
Ermera, 43, 44
European Union Official
    Observer Delegation, 63–4
Evans, Gareth, 5, 98, 130

Falintil, 44–5, 51, 63
Falklands War, 132
Federal elections, Australia
    (1998), 9
Fischer, Jeff, 40, 50, 89–90
Fischer, Judy, 2, 106, 118

France, Jim, 102
Fretilin, 44

Gama, Jaime, 4
Ginangar, Dr, 5–6
Gleno, 43–6, 85, 90, 99,
    100–2, 106, 138
Gough, Phil, 41
Greenlees, Don, 14, 85
Gulf War, 120
Gusmao, Xanana, 12, 27, 78,
    140, 141
Guterres, Eurico, 1, 57

Habibie, President, 9–18, 37,
    60, 116–17
Haider, Rezaqul, 40, 50
Hanson, Pauline, 9
Hayden, Bill, 130
Hayden, Ingrid, 50
Hazel, Geoffrey, 44, 101, 102
Henderson, Noel, 118
Hillary, Edmund, 96
Hoogstad, Nore, 73, 75, 76,
    78, 92
Hosking, Peter, 61
Hotel Dili, 27–8, 53
Hotel Mahkota, 35–7, 77
Hotel Turismo, 24, 31, 41,
    48, 53
Howard, John, letter to
    Habibie, 9–18, 130–1
Hunter, Philip, 100, 102

Indian Ocean Rim Association
    for Regional Cooperation, 64
Indonesia: agrees to popular
    consultation, 3–4; Australia
    gives $1 billion to, 18;
    Commission of Inquiry,
    115; People's Consultative
    Assembly, 5, 49, 117;

plans revenge for pro-independence vote, 116; relations with Australia, 17, 132

Indonesian Army: business activities by generals, 16–17; effect of Asian economic crisis on, 16–17; Kopassus, 26, 30, 115, 116; plans revenge for pro-independence vote, 116; provides minimum security to UNAMET, 105, 122; relations with militias, 103, 115; troops in East Timor, 25

Indonesian Navy, 48

Indonesian police: as security keepers, 34; fail to make arrests, 44; provide minimum security for UNAMET, 105, 117, 122; relations with CIVPOL, 100; relations with militias, 91; revenge for pro-independence vote, 116

INTERFET, 118, 141

internally displaced people, 45

IORARC, 64

Ireland, 8

Isaacs, Leandro, 63

Jacobsen, Craig, 20, 62, 103

Jesuits, 61–2

kangaroo pins, 104

Kitchener, General, 119

Knoth, Max, 100, 102

Kopassus, 26, 30, 115, 116

Korea, 8, 18

Korean War, 120

Kosovo, 121

Kriegler, Johann, 38

Landy, Martin, 58

Lawrence, T.E., 120

Laws, John, 133

Leckie, David, 77, 123, 125–7, 128

Lester, Tim, 36

Leteher, Juan Pablo, 58

Liebmann, Steve, 94

Liquica: Australian Observer Delegation visit to, 32–5, 112; Fischer praises Indonesian police effort in, 104; militia attacks in, 115, 117; militia threats in, 55; Richard Carleton incident, 71–4, 76, 123–4

Llewellyn, Mark, 73, 76

Maliana, 55, 57, 62, 114

Manatuto, 58

Marker, Jamsheed, 39

Martenet, Randy, 102

Martin, Ian, 9, 39, 50–1, 70, 77, 109

Matignon Accords, 12

Mauritius, 137

Maxwell, Robert, 41

McCarthy, John, 13, 22–3, 28, 45, 62, 78, 105

McGregor, Richard, 14

McMullan, Bob, 95

McNamara, Ian, 55

media: at the Hotel Mahkota, 35–7; at the Hotel Turismo, 27–8; Dutch journalist killed, 122; Fischer's relations with, 132–4; interviews with Fischer, 21, 24, 94–5, 106; Irish TV team interrogated by Army, 103; journalists killed at Balibo, 34; on polling day, 69; press conference at UNAMET HQ, 56–7; press conference of Australian Observer Delegation, 84; print journalists examine Carleton's baggage, 95–6; relations with Howard government, 130; reports in Indonesian media, 132; risk of assignment in East Timor, 122–3; role of, 119–34; short history, 119–20; '60 Minutes' debacle, 71–8, 83, 92, 95–6, 106–7, 114–15, 123–9; subgroups within, 121

'Media Watch' (TV program), 129

militias: attack registration centres, 55; attack UNAMET convoy, 34; attack UNAMET headquarters, 99; besiege Gleno, 99, 100–2; command structure and tactics, 60–1; confrontation with 60 Minutes team, 73–4; in Dili, 88–9; feel betrayed by Jakarta, 60; fire on CIVPOL members, 115; hostility towards Australians, 5; intimidation of pro-independence supporters by, 112; killings by, 27; in Liquica, 55, 76, 115, 117; meet Falintil at press conference, 57; post-ballot brutality and destruction, 26, 111, 116–17; relations with

army, 103, 115; relations with police, 91

Mills, Alan, 39, 50, 70, 99–100
Mills, Rob, 102
Molan, Jim, 92
Moore, John, 9–10
Moraitis, Chris, 62
Morris, Paul, 102
Mount Hagen, Papua New Guinea, 43
Muis, Mohamed Noer, 25–6, 55
Mulqueeney, Paul, 117
Murdoch, Lindsay, 28, 84

National Council of the Timorese Resistance, 26, 51, 63, 112
Nazor, Vesna, 36
New Caledonia, 12
New Zealand Observer Delegation, 40–1, 96

O'Callaghan, Jerry, 103
Oakes, Laurie, 95
Oecussi Enclave, 5
oil and gas reserves, Timor Gap, 5–6, 137–8
One Nation, 9

Payne, Marise: arranges briefing on Gleno siege, 99; as member of Australian Observer Delegation, xiii; as Senator, 6; on voting procedures, 82–3, 84; presents Fischer with model steam engine, 107; runs gauntlet at roadblock, 114; visits Balibo and Maliana, 63; visits Baucau, 32

Pearce, Anthony, xiii, 7, 32, 42, 88, 90
Perry, Rae, xiii, 7, 20, 32, 83
Petrie, John, 58
'PM' (radio program), 106
police *see* CIVPOL; Indonesian police
polling day, 66–81
Polres Manatuto District, 58–9
POLRI *see* Indonesian police
Popular Consultation: electoral commissioners, 8, 38–9; origins of term, v; polling day, 66–81; questions on the ballot paper, 108; registration for, 34, 39; result of, 108–9; security on polling day, 34–5, 49, 51
Portugal, 3, 13, 142

referendum *see* Popular Consultation
Relief of Mafeking, 119
Richardson, Graham, 126
Roocke, Justin, 33, 34
Rothschild, Lord, 15–16
Royal Australian Air Force, Darwin base, 20
Ruak, Tauar Matan, 44, 57
Rubio, Carlos, 27–8, 35, 53–4

Santa Cruz Cemetery, 96, 98–9
SBS TV, 77
security personnel, 62–3, 91
Serbia, 121
Shwabsky, Stephanie, xiii, 7, 32, 42, 69
Silaen, Timbul, 25
Singapore, 136–7
'60 Minutes' debacle, 71–8, 83, 92, 95–6, 106–7, 114–15, 123–9

SkyTV, 69
Smith, Michael, 3
Smith, Trevor, 34
Soares, Abilio Jose Osorio, 23
Soares, Constantino, 45–6, 102
Soeharto, President, 16, 17, 19, 64, 65, 97, 117
South Africa, 8
Stations of the Cross, 97–8
Suai, 55
Sukarnoputri, Megawati, 17
Sutton, Ray, 33
Symon, Craig, 56
Symon, Paul, 26, 34, 40, 54–6, 92

Tarmidzi, Agus, 25, 26
Thailand, 18
Thawley, Michael, 13
Thoenes, Sander, 122
Thomas, Lowell, 120
Thompson, Geoff, 36
Timor Gap Treaty, 5–6
TNI *see* Indonesian Army
'Today Show' (TV program), 92–3, 94
tourism, in East Timor, 137

Ular, 45
UNAMET: administers ballot, 7–8, 44, 89, 102, 111, 112–13, 128; Australian involvement in, 70; Carleton fails to register with, 125, 127; collects ballot boxes, 101; convoy attacked by militia, 33–4; creation of, 4; criticisms of, 131; Fischer congratulates, 84; headquarters attacked by militia, 99; initial difficulties with militias, 55;

militias increase
intimidation of, 117–18;
precautions against
retaliation, 106; UNIF
makes allegations against,
109–10
UNIF, 109–10
United Nations Mission in
East Timor *see* UNAMET

Vaile, Mark, 22
Van Klinken, Helene, 44
Vendrell, Francesc, 40
Vietnam War, 120

Wahid, Abdurrahman, 17
Walker, Ignasio, 58

Walsh, Patrick, xiv, 7, 32, 78,
83, 96
War Memorial, 98
Watt, Peter, 102
Wigglesworth, Ann, xiv, 7,
20, 32, 88
Wimhurst, David, 40
Wiranto, General, 15, 60
Wood, Peter, 105
World Bank, 141
World Trade Organisation,
56–7, 135
World War II, 120
Wortel, Johannes, 40

Xavier College, Melbourne, 61
Ximenes, David, 63